Praise

Play Your Big

"This remarkable new book, **Play Your Bigger Game,** is a powerful and brilliant piece of work that will inspire you to live and work in a way that is dynamic and fulfilling. If you are interested in making a difference with your life, if you are committed to living a life of meaning, if you are longing to live your life to the absolute fullest, **Play Your Bigger Game** is a <u>must</u> read. I have been deeply touched by the work of Rick Tamlyn. He is absolute magic. His message is breathing new life into people and organizations all around the world. Buy this book, read it and thrive, and share it with everyone everywhere!"

— LYNNE TWIST,
author of *The Soul of Money,* and cofounder of The Pachamama Alliance

"In this accessible and delightful book, author Rick Tamlyn teaches us that making a difference can be simple, playful, and fun. Tamlyn stimulates, entices, and inspires the Bigger Game player in each of us. **Play Your Bigger Game** is written for that place in each of us that hungers to contribute."

— KAREN KIMSEY-HOUSE,
CEO and co-founder, The Coaches Training Institute, San Rafael, CA

"The Bigger Game is an elegant and effective way to take ideas, dreams, and intangible goals and make them come alive and flourish with purpose. Rick Tamlyn is on to something extraordinary."

— SEAN MAGENNIS,
chief operating officer, YPO-WPO, Irving, TX

"We were fortunate to have Rick present The Bigger Game to our internal team. He was able to shift our mind-set regarding how we work together, recognize that we must play our game every day, and challenge us to see how our game would impact the organization. We still receive comments on how Rick's message strongly resonated with our leaders on a professional and personal level. "During these difficult economic times, it is imperative that each person is able to maximize their effort in order to make the greatest impact, and that all starts with understanding how to **Play Your Bigger Game.**"

— KEVIN MUKHERJEE,
leadership development consultant, national nonprofit organization

*"**Play Your Bigger Game** is about connecting dots from the past to the present and to the future. The Bigger Game takes you from an 'it's about me' perspective to an 'it's about us' perspective and empowers each of us to live a Bigger Game life and create shared value."*

— HYUNSOOK KIM,
Bigger Game trainer and representative, Seoul, South Korea

"I watched the impact of a Bigger Game workshop launch an IBM sales team from last to first in the organization. And it was so much more than just sales volume. Their game was to bring success to their customers.
"I was their internal sales consultant and watched the team create innovative customer solutions and develop their employees to be their best. The more the leaders played their game, the more successful they became! Customers were delighted and employee satisfaction was high. They became the team everyone wanted to be on. And even as the core Bigger Game team members were offered new opportunities, they left as players—committed to spreading the message. The Bigger Game was life and career changing."

— SARA SMITH,
IBM sales transformation manager, Fort Worth, TX

*"I passionately embarked on my Bigger Game journey when first introduced to its technology. I was so inspired that I fervently spread The Bigger Game concepts to colleagues, executives, and teams, enabling me to witness others birth new possibilities when they united on common Bigger Games. If your soul is stirring for purpose, adventure, and/or transformation, choose **Play Your Bigger Game** as your trustworthy escort."*

— SUSAN VALDISERRI,
president, Leaders of Purpose, Inc., Chicago, IL

"The Bigger Game model offers a powerful road map to fulfillment. It can be used in so many ways—to discover where you are, or to nudge you into that next bold step in pursuit of your dreams. Because it is authentic, it is universally applicable."

— LEZA DANLY,
founder, Lucid Living, Novato, CA

PLAY
YOUR
BIGGER
GAME

Hay House Titles of Related Interest

YOU CAN HEAL YOUR LIFE, the movie,
starring Louise L. Hay & Friends
(available as a 1-DVD program and an expanded 2-DVD set)
Watch the trailer at: **www.LouiseHayMovie.com**

THE SHIFT, the movie,
starring Dr. Wayne W. Dyer
(available as a 1-DVD program and an expanded 2-DVD set)
Watch the trailer at: **www.DyerMovie.com**

✪ ✪ ✪

AUTHENTIC SUCCESS:
Essential Lessons and Practices from the World's
Leading Coaching Program on Success Intelligence,
by Robert Holden, Ph.D.

THE COMPASSIONATE SAMURAI:
Being Extraordinary in an Ordinary World,
by Brian Klemmer

INNER VOICE:
Unlock Your Purpose and Passion,
by Russ Whitney

INSPIRED DESTINY:
Living a Fulfilling and Purposeful Life,
by Dr. John F. Demartini

YOUR DESTINY SWITCH:
Master Your Key Emotions, and Attract the Life of Your Dreams!,
by Peggy McColl

All of the above are available at your local bookstore,
or may be ordered by visiting:

Hay House USA: **www.hayhouse.com**®
Hay House Australia: **www.hayhouse.com.au**
Hay House UK: **www.hayhouse.co.uk**
Hay House South Africa: **www.hayhouse.co.za**
Hay House India: **www.hayhouse.co.in**

PLAY
YOUR
BIGGER
GAME

9 MINUTES TO LEARN, A LIFETIME TO LIVE

RICK TAMLYN

HAY HOUSE, INC.
Carlsbad, California • New York City
London • Sydney • Johannesburg
Vancouver • New Delhi

Published and distributed in the United States by: Hay House, Inc.: www.hayhouse.
com® • *Published and distributed in Australia by:* Hay House Australia Pty. Ltd.: www.
hayhouse.com.au • *Published and distributed in the United Kingdom by:* Hay House
UK, Ltd.: www.hayhouse.co.uk • *Published and distributed in the Republic of South
Africa by:* Hay House SA (Pty), Ltd.: www.hayhouse.co.za • *Distributed in Canada by:*
Raincoast: www.raincoast.com • *Published in India by:* Hay House Publishers India:
www.hayhouse.co.in

Cover design: Karla Baker • *Interior design:* Charles McStravick

Library of Congress Cataloging-in-Publication Data

Tamlyn, Rick.
 Play your bigger game : 9 minutes to learn, a lifetime to live / Rick Tamlyn.
    pages cm
  ISBN 978-1-4019-4294-6 (pbk.)
 1. Self-actualization (Psychology) I. Title.
 BF637.S4T36 2013
 158.1--dc23
                                        2013023624

ISBN: 978-1-4019-4294-6

10 9 8 7 6 5 4 3
1st edition, October 2013

SUSTAINABLE
FORESTRY
INITIATIVE
Certified Chain of Custody
Promoting Sustainable Forestry
www.sfiprogram.org
SFI-01268
SFI label applies to the text stock

PRINTED IN THE UNITED STATES OF AMERICA

My friend and co-creator Laura Whitworth was the ultimate Bigger Game player, one who had an uncanny ability to inspire people to step up as leaders and have a greater impact in the world. I am blessed to have been one of those she touched and inspired. Laura woke me to my potential and called me forth to take The Bigger Game message to a global audience. Driven to a great degree by her fiery passion, we co-created this simple yet profound model of motivation. Laura was also co-founder of The Coaches Training Institute and co-author of <u>Co-Active Coaching,</u> one of the world's most influential books on leadership and life coaching. Laura passed away on February 28, 2007, after a long and courageous battle with lung cancer. I still miss her fierce and bold voice, but her memory still serves to stir and ignite my passion, and deepen my sense of purpose. Laura's intellect, empathy, and zest for life live on in this book and in every subsequent Bigger Game player. Thank you, dear friend!

CONTENTS

INTRODUCTION

Why Play Your Bigger Game?

Melissa O'Mara and Alice Coles have little in common at first glance. Melissa has a college degree and has spent most of her career in high-level management positions in Fortune 500 corporations. Alice Coles is a single mother who toiled as a crab picker, earning just $5,000 a year while living in one of the most impoverished and neglected rural communities in the nation.

You may be surprised to learn, however, that both Melissa and Alice are skilled and avid players of The Bigger Game. Alice, in fact, may be the more celebrated bigger game player of the two women. Her incredible successes as a community activist and advocate for the rural poor have been highlighted on *60 Minutes* and other major media outlets.

Both women are major game changers in their respective areas of influence. Melissa has quietly led the green movement from within corporate America. Alice simply saved and rebuilt most of her once-squalid community in a relentless and still-ongoing campaign that has become a model and inspiration for grassroots activists around the world.

As the co-founder of The Bigger Game, I've worked with both of these phenomenal women, and I'm in awe of their determination, intelligence, and resourcefulness. I'll share the specifics of their bigger games and those of many others in this book. But first, I'd like to offer one thought for you to keep in mind as you read the pages that follow: this book is personal, and it's about *you* setting something great in motion.

Like Melissa and Alice, you may not know exactly what you are hungering for right now. Don't worry about that. Just go with the fact that in picking up this book, you've acknowledged that you are searching for something more.

Isaac Newton's first law of motion states, "An object at rest stays at rest, and an object in motion stays in motion." In the same way, we humans tend to keep doing what we're doing. Our natural tendency is to resist change. This results in a state known as *inertia,* which is the tendency to do nothing.

The Bigger Game is your antidote to inertia. It's meant to put your life in motion and to keep it in motion. One of the biggest promises of playing your own game is that you'll never feel "stuck" for long.

To be a player, you don't have to have your game all figured out. You don't even need a name for it. You just need to get rolling. Momentum will take care of the rest. The Bigger Game greases your wheels.

Once you begin playing your own bigger game, something organic happens. You give up the need to control and strategize everything. It's not that controlling and strategizing are bad and organic is good, but controlling and strategizing are tasks conducted from the left side of the brain (logic), and sometimes we need to lean a little more to the right side (creativity). The Bigger Game is similar to Mother Nature. Both are forces greater than any one of us. Our best bet is to adapt as we go, ride the wave, and follow the flow.

IT'S ALL MADE UP

The Bigger Game is a concept that will take you only nine minutes to understand and a lifetime to play. It was designed from the premise that life itself is one big game that's all made up. Your life is what you make it to be.

So, if life is a game and it's all made up, why not play a game of your own design—one that excites you, challenges you, and allows you to fully express your talents and creativity?

By the way, there's nothing wrong with hungering for such a passionate existence. It's a natural expression of who we are. Since each of us is blessed with talents, we are naturally hungry to develop them and put them to use.

Too often we suppress that desire for full engagement and self-expression, because we think that's the grown-up thing to do. We consciously turn down our hunger dials, because we're afraid of expecting too much. We also think, *If I settle for less, I will then avoid being disappointed.*

The Bigger Game was created to counteract the self-limiting, fear-based approach to life. Michelangelo said, "The great danger for most of us lies not in setting our aim too high and falling short, but in setting our aim too low and hitting the mark."

The Bigger Game is not just about making a living; it's about creating an impact. Interestingly enough, I find that once players begin to make a positive impact, their incomes often rise, too.

Still, if you're interested simply in making a living and just surviving in life, I'm afraid this book and The Bigger Game are not for you. If you're interested in making your mark and thriving through the full expression of all of your gifts and blessings, please read on.

The purpose of this book is to do the following:

✶ Reveal The Bigger Game player that you already are.

✶ Help you find The Bigger Game(s) that excites and challenges you to fully deploy all of your energy and gifts.

✶ Teach you to consciously design the person you are destined to become.

✶ Allow you to feed the hunger in your soul.

✶ Help you to make a major impact and to leave a lasting legacy.

You should play The Bigger Game if you:

✶ Want to have a more positive impact within your family, your work, your community, or your organization

✖ Yearn for meaningful work that matters

✖ Long to be more innovative

✖ Seek to be more collaborative

✖ Hunger for a change but aren't sure what sort of change

✖ Are looking for more than an "okay" life or a business-as-usual existence

✖ Want to take responsibility and direct your destiny

✖ Aspire to make a difference or leave a legacy

✖ Are ready to become a leader

✖ Have had enough of sitting in the stands as an observer

THIS IS NOT BUSINESS AS USUAL

Just what is it that will make you, your group, your organization, or your community successful? Most experts agree that success comes to those individuals or groups whose hunger for something better attracts allies who share a compelling vision.

Unfortunately, those who deal with the day-to-day reality of demanding jobs and busy families tend to fall into the business-as-usual mode. We accept lower levels of accomplishment, unfulfilling careers, and even mediocre performance. We tend to do business as usual until the business goes bust.

I co-created The Bigger Game with the late Laura Whitworth, the co-founder of The Coaches Training Institute, where I've studied and taught. Our goal was to create a remedy for "business as usual." After Laura's death from cancer in 2007, I grieved for more than a year. But eventually, I was compelled to continue our work to honor her memory. Since then, I've traveled the world coaching and training tens of thousands of people across all walks of life, groups within the corporate world and nonprofit organizations, as well as individuals.

The Bigger Game uses a traditional game board that resembles the classic tic-tac-toe game as a playful method for helping individuals, leaders, teams, and organizations achieve great things, not out of obligation but because they're driven by a deep and meaningful, compelling purpose.

The Bigger Game offers an engaging and highly effective system for innovating and evolving as individuals, groups, or organizations. The method, when passionately applied, helps individuals and groups intentionally define what they want to accomplish and who they want to become within their families, communities, environments, or careers.

Those who play The Bigger Game say it helps them satiate their hunger for fulfillment while allowing them to serve a higher purpose and to find deeper meaning, rather than allowing circumstances to dictate their behaviors and the course of their lives.

We want our lives to have meaning. We don't want to settle for mere survival. So dare to be hungry.

Transform your life into a bold statement of purpose and empowerment. You don't want to have regrets when you look back upon it.

Apple CEO Steve Jobs addressed that hunger in his remarkable 2005 speech to new graduates at Stanford: "Your time is limited, so don't waste it living someone else's life. Don't be trapped by dogma—which is living with the results of other people's thinking. Don't let the noise of others' opinions drown out your own inner voice. And most important, have the courage to follow your heart and intuition. They somehow already know what you truly want to become. Everything else is secondary."

Once you decide to play The Bigger Game, the simple act of being in the flow of it designs who you want to become. You become immersed in the process before you have time to think or plan how to do it.

One of the underlying philosophies of The Bigger Game is that goals are overrated. Whether you're a student, a recent graduate, a professional in midcareer, an executive, an entrepreneur, or a seeker of greater meaning and fulfillment, the game provides the space where your creativity flows naturally and innovation is an authentic product of your engagement.

A couple housekeeping points: For the sake of learning the model and understanding the methodology, I suggest reading this entire book first and then coming back to certain chapters for further reference as you create and play your bigger game. Feel free to keep a journal to capture your thoughts as you read and play.

You've probably already noticed that I capitalize The Bigger Game when referring to the concept, but not when referring to the bigger games of individuals or players in general. It's sort of like Major League Baseball and a baseball game, one is the overarching concept and brand while the other is an individual or team pursuit.

When you are fully engaged in your own bigger game, which will be something that truly matters, you discover that goals are met and problems solved as you play. Instead of holding meetings and worrying about how to accomplish a goal, you do it as part of the process. Your attention isn't focused on outcomes; it's focused on playing.

When you discover your bigger game, you find yourself compelled from the inside out. If you spend your life doing what you're naturally drawn and driven to do, then the rewards are there for you every day, not just at the end of the day. You see, it's not all about winning the game; it's about the playing.

No one has to tell you when to show up for work or what to do at work. Your work lives inside you as your purpose. It's personal, and, as a result, your energy level soars. You find yourself performing at unprecedented levels: doing more, achieving more, creating fresh opportunities, and feeling more fulfilled.

To play, you must be willing to examine whether you are truly fulfilled in your current game. In my workshops, I often encounter panicked participants who say, "But I have to make my division's numbers next quarter. I don't have time for a bigger game."

There's no play in that mentality. There's very little room for introspection and self-assessment in goal obsession. If you have no interest in leaving your comfort zone, even if you're not all that comfortable, then this game is not for you.

The Bigger Game is designed to create a paradigm and perspective shift for an individual, a team, or an organization. Yet, when the game is played passionately, those shifts occur naturally and in the flow of full engagement. This shift is not forced. You can't force a true paradigm and perspective shift. Yet, the recession and global financial crisis that began in 2006 had many companies in panic mode, demanding, "We need innovation now!"

As you might imagine, that sort of stressful environment is not conducive to innovation and creativity. The Bigger Game gives birth to innovation naturally, because it's a form of play in which the focus isn't on outcomes or problem solving. Instead, solutions and innovations result from the process of creating a new way of living and working.

A GAME FOR ALL

Melissa O'Mara is just one example of individuals whom I've supported and coached to find their bigger games over the last 15 years. Many of them work within major corporations. Others are big thinkers and entrepreneurs in the public sector, nonprofits, religious organizations, and every field imaginable. Their shared compelling purpose is to be fully engaged and fulfilled in work that also makes a difference in their communities and in the world around them. You can never be too small or too big to play The Bigger Game, which is an expression of your self in the world that, in some way, makes a positive difference. The word *bigger* is not related to size and volume but, rather, applies to stepping up to create something so compelling and with such passion that your engagement in life will expand exponentially. If we're not evolving, we're devolving. Playing a Bigger Game will guarantee evolution and, in some cases, even revolution.

I introduced Melissa to The Bigger Game in a corporate workshop, and over a period of a few years, she participated in several more of my presentations. Once Melissa zeroed in on her own bigger game, she proved to be an avid player. She'd spent 16 years in sales and management at IBM. Smart and dynamic, Melissa thrived, but when she paused long enough to notice it, she frequently felt a hunger for something more.

She had navigated her career in a way that enabled her to continuously learn, and yet, she'd reached a point where she yearned for work that had a greater impact, something that resonated beyond the corporate environment.

Like thousands of others hungering for greater meaning in their careers and lives, Melissa found what she was looking for by playing The Bigger Game. "The Bigger Game gave me a context for how I could leverage the corporate platform to do important and fulfilling work in the larger world," said Melissa, whose story I'll explore in greater depth later in the book.

When you do express yourself through good work, the world responds by sending abundance and blessings your way. It's not about doing and getting; it's about expressing and receiving. Playing The Bigger Game takes you out of surviving mode and puts you in thriving mode. Like Melissa O'Mara, your bigger game will transform you from a worker to a player—on a scale greater than any you've ever imagined!

Once you decide to play The Bigger Game—even if you don't yet know what your game is or how to create it—the simple act of being in the flow of it designs the person you want to become, and that takes you where you want to go. You become immersed in the process before you have time to think or plan how to do it.

When you're fully engaged in your own bigger game, the *how* becomes irrelevant. Your attention isn't focused on outcomes, because you're so engaged in the process. Your goals are met and problems are solved in the flow of playing the game.

Are you ready to live fully by expressing *your* bigger game?

If so, let your game begin!

● ✖ ●

PART I

NAME YOUR GAME

HOW THE BIGGER GAME FOUND ME

When I was growing up, my family belonged to the Old Paramus Reformed Church in Ridgewood, New Jersey. Ours was an activist church with very positive energy, which filtered down to the youth group. Both of my older brothers served as youth-group leaders in their high-school days, so I was thrilled when Rev. Staver and my fellow classmates voted me in as president of the Senior Youth Group.

Since I was following in my big brothers' footsteps, I told the pastor I wanted to make a mark by doing something that had never been done before. I had no idea what that "something" might be. I just wanted to pull off a feat more memorable and more impactful than the usual bowling party or spaghetti-dinner fund-raiser.

Years later, I would realize that this was my first experience with the guiding concept and principles behind The Bigger Game. I had a hunger to do something outside the norm and take a bold action based on a compelling purpose. Allies were lined up. I wanted to build upon what my brothers and previous youth-group presidents had done and make a meaningful difference.

The pastor and I brainstormed back and forth for a few days before we came up with what I later realized was my first bigger game. For years, the youth group had held fund-raisers for one of our mission churches located in the impoverished Appalachian region of Kentucky. Rev. Staver suggested that instead of just sending money to them, we could go there to help these beautiful souls of Annville, Kentucky.

"Let's do it," I said.

Then all we had to do was figure out how to raise enough money to transport 32 kids and their chaperones a distance of over 500 miles, feed them, house them, and find useful things for them to do in a region of the country as foreign as Mars to a bunch of suburban New Jersey teens.

Was it a little more complicated than staging yet another Strawberry Shortcake Festival in the church parking lot? Definitely. Yet, one of the secrets of finding your bigger game is that you feel so compelled and so engaged that you focus on the process of accomplishing the mission.

When a sense of mission overtakes you and a sense of passion drives you or your group, the focus is so powerful and the energy so positive that you don't need to know the *how*. You just figure it out as you go. Motivation is not a problem. You're driven from the inside out. Instead of sitting around fretting and pondering, you tap your creative energy and move forward—over, under, around, and through obstacles. In fact, obstacles can actually become a source of inspiration; I'll share more about that later on.

We had no idea how to accomplish our mission, but we were committed to making the trip. Over the next few months, we raised money at car washes and bake sales, and had, for the very first time, a 24-hour dance marathon sponsored by our church. We recruited adult allies of all types: carpenters, plumbers, electricians, and other craftspeople to join the team and to teach us home-building and repair skills. We also raised a substantial sum of money through donations.

I learned so much in the process. One of the most important discoveries was that I could be a leader. Each week, I had to give a progress report at our youth-group meetings. Somehow, out of chaos, we created order. We had help from the pastor and other adults, especially Vic and Wilma Egg, our youth-group advisors, but they gave us plenty of room to make mistakes and learn from them. Vic and Wilma became true co-players in this bigger game, stepping outside of their own comfort zones and becoming my role models for doing good in our world. I spent many hours pouring out my soul to them, and they kindly nurtured me. Our team of teens quickly transformed into a well-oiled, mission-making machine because of our hunger for this project.

Thirty-six of us made the trip to the Appalachian community of about 500 people. These amazing and loving folks were hungry for assistance of all kinds. They welcomed us into their homes, some of which had no electricity or running water. We then set to work, under the supervision of our adult teammates, and did whatever we could to improve the lives of those people. In return, they shared their stories and their homes with us, teaching us about a culture and a place we might never have known otherwise. They taught me what it means to love and what it means to be committed to family and faith, lessons that live in me to this day and will do so till my last breath.

Their gratitude and acceptance was a great gift, one that every member of our group still carries decades later. I think we made a difference in their lives. I know they made a difference in ours. My experiences with them were a major inspiration for the bigger game that has become my life's work.

One of the joys of playing your bigger game is that it generates rewards and results beyond anything you could have imagined when you began. Wondrous and powerful forces are set in motion when you find a compelling purpose and take bold action despite your fears. The momentum you create by stepping out of your comfort zone keeps building, changing your life, and, probably, the lives of everyone you meet.

Our youth-group mission to Appalachia gave me a sense of fulfillment unlike anything I'd ever known. Upon our return to New Jersey, the church elders invited me to speak about our mission to the entire congregation. I worked up a speech and a slide show (PowerPoint hadn't been invented yet). But when I stood at the church lectern, the words that I'd prepared went out the window. I spoke directly from my heart instead. I didn't know it at the time, but I was swept up in the power of a compelling purpose.

Members of the congregation laughed and cried along with me as I passionately described the work we'd done, the people we'd met, and how touched and inspired we'd been by our trip.

I'd never felt so alive. We had created an incredible life-changing experience from just an idea. We had no plan for how to pull it off, yet we accomplished our "game" with amazing efficiency. All that planning and effort never felt like work. I was caught up in a creative flow, fully engaged and in the moment. Honestly, I had no idea what I was experiencing, but whatever was going on, I wanted more of it. Years later, it would dawn on me that I was just then beginning a journey that my father had long encouraged me to embark upon, one that would allow me to never feel "stuck" or unfulfilled.

LOOKING TO CREATE A GREAT RIDE

My father instilled in me a hunger for a fulfilling and meaningful life. Dad was a lively, funny person who probably would have made a great comedian, but instead he worked in human resources for General Motors. His was not always a fulfilling job. There were many frustrations for him, but he was driven by the promise of a comfortable retirement.

That didn't happen. A few years before his retirement date, the pension package was changed such that he received not nearly what he'd planned on. My father was disappointed in the way things turned out. In his later years, he often told my brothers and me that we should design our lives around doing something we loved, something with a compelling purpose. He helped us realize that the focus of our lives shouldn't be making it to retirement age; what counted were the experiences along the way, the fulfillment found in the journey itself.

"At the end of your life, you want to look back and say, 'That was a great ride,' rather than, 'I wish I'd done something else,'" he'd tell us.

All parents hope that their children won't make the same mistakes they made. I'm sure they also hope that their children will find a smoother path than their own. I'm sure it wasn't easy for Dad to admit to me that he was somewhat disappointed in the way his life turned out, but I admire and appreciate that he wanted something better for my brothers and me. He was deeply proud of being a great provider and inspiring father to his three sons, all of whom are now living passionate lives. Thank you, Dad. His shared lesson stayed with me. For the longest time, I lived by those words without even consciously being aware of their source.

Like most children, of course, I forged my own, crooked path. My dad was in the human resources department, and I didn't stray far afield. The Bigger Game is all about making the most of human capital, which history has shown to be the greatest of all resources on this planet. But at first, I set out to be an actor and entertainer, and I struggled in the grand tradition of aspiring thespians everywhere.

I had majored in communications as an undergraduate but had no clue what I wanted to do for the rest of my life upon graduation. Amazingly, I auditioned for a summer-stock theater company at my college and was cast in five shows. It was this experience that activated a deep hunger to want to entertain and engage people on the stage. This hunger came from the inside out, and so I was driven to satisfy it.

Without giving any thought to the fact that I had no real training or experience, I applied to graduate theater programs at several colleges. The University of Connecticut was among those that offered me an audition. I put together two monologues and a song, and apparently, they weren't bad. They gave me almost a full scholarship, another confirmation that life is all made up and that we need to just go for it without knowing *how*.

After three years of performing in college productions and in summer stock, I graduated and moved to New York City.

I found steady but low-paying work, with bit parts as an extra in television soap operas, including *One Life to Live* and *Guiding Light*. I also appeared in a couple of commercials for Disney's Queen Mary cruise ship and performed off-off-Broadway—okay, Connecticut—and won a couple of awards in theaters there.

I did do a spin on Broadway, but it was as a waiter at Cirella's Italian Restaurant. I lived on the Upper West Side, packed into a two-bedroom apartment with three other fabulous struggling actor-waiters, enjoying every minute of big-city life.

Then, after five years in New York City, I accepted an invitation from an agent who wanted me to move to Los Angeles and give movies a try. Like the minor-league ballplayer who moves to the majors, I was suddenly competing with the elite in my field. Everyone seemed to be better looking, more talented, and more insanely driven—not to mention more tanned.

For New York actors, the theater is a shared passion, and most actors were mutually supportive. Hollywood's film industry is more of a business—or an addictive drug that people would kill for. The competition was fierce and the cost of living high, so I went looking for another "day job." Through friends, I learned about a new restaurant opening in Beverly Hills. I didn't have a phone number, so I went without an appointment, hoping to get an interview for a waiter job. I was wearing a tie, sport coat, and khaki pants. I was 29 years old and needed a job, so it seemed wise to show up in the standard-issue "Please hire me!" uniform.

I'd forgotten that this was laid-back California, not uptight New York. Apparently, I was the only applicant to show up with a knot at his throat. I walked into the restaurant, which was under construction, and a friendly and engaging woman asked me what I was looking for.

"A job," I said.

This woman, Linda Candioty, who started as a test baker and then became The Cheesecake Factory's first hostess and later rose to become an executive vice president, was in charge of hiring. She told me the restaurant didn't need any more waiters, but then she hired me anyway.

"I was sort of done hiring, but when a guy shows up in a sports coat and tie for a waitstaff job in Beverly Hills, I want that guy in my restaurant," Linda explained to me years later, after we'd become better friends.

Actually, it was David Overton's restaurant. Again, I didn't know it at the time, but David was truly a bigger game player. The novice restaurateur was building his tiny place in Beverly Hills upon his mother's prowess as a cheesecake baker. Linda and I were among his first group of employees at their newly expanded Beverly Hills restaurant. David's parents, Oscar and Evelyn, had operated small bakeries and restaurants in Detroit and, later, Los Angeles, so they had laid the groundwork for their son's Beverly Hills shop, which in turn became the launchpad for one of the most successful bigger games in the dining business: The Cheesecake Factory, which now has more than 170 locations worldwide. And they are now beginning to expand into the Middle East, Mexico, and Latin America. The Cheesecake Factory game grows bigger with each expansion!

I didn't realize it at the time, but joining the start-up team at The Cheesecake Factory would prove to be my second exposure to many of the basic principles and concepts that would come together in the creation of The Bigger Game. Here are a few of those that I've embraced:

* Let your hunger be your guide to create what compels you. David Overton trusted his intuition and followed his passion into the restaurant business. One of my favorite quotes is: "Uncertainty is caused by a lack of knowledge. Hesitation is the product of fear." David may have been uncertain about how to be a successful restaurateur, but he did not hesitate, because he was compelled deeply.

* His compelling purpose was personal. It was his parents' business so he was deeply invested. I believe a compelling purpose must be personal. No one else can assign one to you. It has to be from your heart.

* The whole is greater then the sum of its parts. The Cheesecake Factory organization puts attention on every detail of the dining experience. It is not a meal, it truly is a "bigger game" dining experience.

* Invest in your people. My training as a waitstaff member was more thorough than anything I'd experienced on the job. Their investment in me made me want to be a great team member. It was a win-win because my training made me a great employee. I earned substantial income from tips, which paid for my training as an actor.

* Build it and they will come. David had a unique vision. He built according to that vision, and people flocked to it in droves. He did not hide in the comfort zone of "What if no one likes it?" Even better, he built his company responsibly, nurturing his employees and his products with great attention to detail, and the business, his team, and their customers were rewarded.

David Overton lived those principles and concepts. His mother made her first cheesecake from a recipe in a newspaper and had given it to her husband's boss, who asked her to make a dozen more so that he could give them as Christmas gifts. Before she knew it, Evelyn Overton was in the cheesecake business, making them in her Detroit basement. Husband Oscar delivered them to local restaurants for resale. Son David earned a penny for every cake box he folded.

As a teenager, David was more into drums than desserts. He and his band were lured west to the flourishing hippie rock-music scene in San Francisco. Later, his parents moved to California, too, settling in the Los Angeles area, where they opened a wholesale cheesecake business. After a few years, David gave up on his rock 'n' roll dreams and joined his parents in their San Fernando Valley shop. His mother's cheesecakes had such a strong following that David decided to open a restaurant featuring her baked goods.

David considered his mom's creations to be the "Cadillac of cheesecakes," so he targeted one of the most upscale dining markets in the world: Beverly Hills. With an investment of $125,000 from family and friends, David opened his first restaurant in 1978. He kept the main courses simple with basics like roast chicken and hamburgers, because he couldn't make more elaborate entrées. His mother's cheesecake desserts were the big draw, and immediately the Beverly Hills restaurant had long waiting lines.

I joined the waitstaff at the original Cheesecake Factory just as they were expanding. They opened four more locations in California and Washington, D.C., before Oscar and Evelyn retired. David then took the company public in 1992 to fund more expansion, which led to years of steady growth and profits even through the recession. The company's annual profits are now more than $98.4 million on sales of $1.8 billion.

Cheesecake Factory restaurants now anchor major malls and shopping areas across the nation and around the world. David Overton is known for having some of the keenest taste buds and one of the sharpest minds in the food business. Nothing goes on the menu without his personal approval. He also has succeeded in a very challenging and competitive field with a unique approach that's both spiritual and humanistic.

I can attest to the fact that David's management style has worked well for him and the many people who staff his restaurants. David is a natural born bigger game player. He encourages everyone to approach life with an abundance mentality and the belief that anything is possible.

Most business owners, for example, fear competition and keep it at bay as best they can. David always welcomed other restaurants when they moved in near his own. His belief is that our customers benefited from the presence of other restaurants, because often we were so busy that some customers couldn't be served quickly enough to meet their needs. He was glad to have other restaurants nearby to handle our overflow.

David also cared about his team. He always told his waitstaff that he knew we were working in the service industry on our way to something grander. His goal was to help us along the way. He'd tell us that he wanted us to make as much money as we could while on the job, and he encouraged us to chase our dreams as actors, musicians, dancers, writers, or whatever our passions might be.

Linda Candioty is an outstanding example of someone who grew within an organization while playing her own bigger game of providing superior customer experiences. She rose from the company's first restaurant hostess to executive vice president, in part because of her amazing gift for "guest" strategies and incredibly thorough employee-training programs. I studied flash cards for weeks so I could pass the "final exam" that every waiter was required to take. When I started there, we had to know every ingredient in each of the 100 items offered on what was then a 17-page menu.

Linda gave us the tools to handle any and every situation, including how to work with customers when something was wrong with a meal or the service. We learned to listen and empathize with our guests. She also taught us to never be afraid to admit mistakes, and we were empowered to buy a round of cheesecake slices (after asking a manager, of course) for a table to set things right whenever necessary.

Our goal was for each guest to walk out the door with a smile and good feelings about dining with us. Efficiency was also a focus. I was making a cappuccino for a guest one night at the wait station, when I looked up and saw Linda observing me.

"There are too many steps in our process for making cappuccino, aren't there?" she asked.

I agreed that it was a time-consuming process. Together, we worked out a new approach that involved moving the cappuccino cups four inches to the right so I could use both hands and speed up the process. I found the overall approach to guest service and employee benefits so appealing that after nine years as a waiter at The Cheesecake Factory, I was promoted to its employee-training team.

We trained the cooks, chefs, and waitstaff for four months at our first Washington, D.C., area restaurant. It had the most seating we'd ever offered and a prime location. We held a "soft" opening with no advertising or fanfare on a Tuesday at 11:00 A.M. The only indication that we were opening was a tiny sign placed in the window. Within 40 minutes, our hungry guests besieged us. The only time it slowed down was when we closed the doors that night.

By the following Saturday, there was a three-and-a-half-hour wait time for dinner.

As a manager, I ran like crazy, trying to keep the guests happy and the service as efficient as possible. I commanded a wait station, and at one point, I looked up to see the boss, Mr. Cheesecake himself, coming toward me. David was taking it all in and looking pleased.

He was not one to jump up and down and cheer. David is a serene person, very Zenlike.

"What's the secret of getting such an amazing response within just a few days of opening?" I asked.

"The whole is greater than the sum of its parts," he said with a smile.

David knew that if we got the details right, if every staffer knew every aspect of the business and exactly what was expected, the restaurant would come together and our guests would be happy. The result of his meticulous attention to detail and devotion to service is a bigger game that has become one of the biggest restaurant successes in the world.

STILL HUNGRY

Meanwhile during all that time, I was working with an amazing coach whom I had met in New York at an organization called the Actors Information Project (AIP). My coach with AIP was Cynthia Loy Darst. We met each week, and she guided me in dealing with contracts, agents, lawyers, taxes, and other necessary evils. Cynthia also took an interest in my personal development, which was of great value to me. At one point after moving to Los Angeles, I asked her how she'd learned to be such an empathetic coach, and she told me about The Coaches Training Institute (CTI), where she'd taken workshops.

After I'd become a trainer with The Cheesecake Factory, Cynthia suggested I take a CTI workshop, too. That ultimately led to my life's work, but first I did a four-year stint in corporate America. I enjoyed the restaurant business. I just wasn't sure it was the best use of my talents. I was still acting, and to support that "habit" I began working in temp jobs to get a taste of other career fields. One of those assignments was in marketing for Korn/Ferry International (K/FI), the global executive-search firm. Within a few weeks of my being a temp worker there, they offered me a full-time job, and I accepted. This was another moment of, "Wow, look! How did that happen?"

There, I learned a great deal about what's demanded of leaders and teams at the highest levels of business. As I look back at this time at K/FI, I realize the company was the perfect ally to set me up for what was coming next.

I left K/FI to launch my own career in the coaching and leadership-development field. The classes I'd taken at CTI, along with my experiences at The Cheesecake Factory and K/FI, gave me a vision for a path that would allow me to make a difference in the careers and lives of men and women in both the private and corporate sectors.

I began attending CTI in its early years. It would grow to become one of the largest and most respected training school for coaches in the world. My instructor was Karen Kimsey-House, whose (eventual) husband, Henry, had co-founded CTI with Karen and Laura Whitworth. Their work was focused on developing professional coaches who could help people find fulfillment, balance, and joy in each moment life provided them.

My acting career had been enjoyable, but it wasn't providing the stability or security I wanted for my life. Karen helped me see the potential for a more stable and fulfilling career path as a life and career coach. I went on to take every course offered at CTI. Eventually I became a trainer in their coaching classes, later a trainer of their trainers, and then a senior trainer in their amazing leadership program.

The timing proved to be perfect. Back then, most people were familiar with therapists and counselors who helped with psychological and emotional issues, but there was an unmet need for assistance in personal development and career fulfillment. The personal coaching and training industry addressed those needs using principles of positive psychology. Well-trained coaches help individuals move forward in their daily lives. There was and remains a great hunger for this service, and CTI is now a global organization.

I still do training and leadership-development courses for CTI, which opened the door to my own bigger game. Coaching and training gave me the chance to engage with people beyond anything I'd experienced as an actor. Henry Kimsey-House told me, "Rick, your job is to breathe life into people and their plans." I loved that! It gave me a compelling purpose and enriched my life. This was especially important given my father's constant encouragement to make my life "a great ride" rather than to end it with regrets.

A GREATER PURPOSE

By the late 1990s, I was a veteran member of the team at CTI. In our many discussions, co-founder Laura Whitworth and I realized that we shared a vision for taking the coaching business into a new realm. She had even put a name to the dream and developed a deceptively simple model that made it easily adaptable for real-world application.

The concept Laura came up with was actually born behind bars. She and some fellow CTI coaches had been contracted by a prison to teach life-coaching skills to Denver inmates. Her goal was to train them to help each other prepare for better lives. To accomplish that mission, Laura wanted to incorporate the basic elements of CTI's program in a model that was easy to grasp and apply. This prison coaching initiative was originally called The Bigger Game Project.

The challenges of creating this program were considerable. Prison officials were skeptical, and as you might imagine, so were the inmates. Laura and her team boldly took on the project without a clue as to how they would pull it off. She realized this was way out of her comfort zone. She'd hungered to do something meaningful and long lasting, yet she felt both compelled and scared as she invested many hours of work into creating it, with the help of other believers.

Although I was not a part of this prison bigger game, I was very much an ally for Laura as we had many long discussions about all of the conflicting feelings and varied elements that went into the creative mix. We talked about stepping outside comfort zones, hungering for something bigger than you know how to do, and the power of a compelling purpose that drives you past your fears and into bold actions. This all resonated with me because of my own experiences dating back to our church youth group's Appalachia project, insights I'd gained working for David Overton and the "bigger game" restaurant empire he'd created, and what I'd observed working with Korn/ Ferry and its senior-level executive clientele. Themes kept emerging that eventually became a part of The Bigger Game methodology and philosophy.

Together, in her living room over several days, we created The Bigger Game. As our program unfolded and evolved, Laura and I talked about using The Bigger Game as a leadership coaching method in a much larger context.

From those discussions, I found my life's work. Laura sensed a need for "something more" out there. That need seemed to increase dramatically after the horrendous events of September 11, 2001. She and I watched the terrorist attacks unfold on TV while we were attending a CTI company-wide meeting.

After witnessing the worst of humanity, we had a fire in our bellies to come up with a world-changing program that brought out the best in people. She and I were so compelled that the concepts and language came together like never before. We strived to find a method for creating lifelong inner conversations that engage individuals while fostering awareness, collaboration, insights, and a powerful sense of purpose.

In late 2001, Laura and I collaborated in our own training and organizational development business. Our goal was to take a much more refined version of The Bigger Game into corporate America and organizations around the world. We had great success initially, working with IBM, one of the world's biggest corporate brands, as our first major client.

Tragically, over the next six years, Laura, a recovering heavy smoker, became seriously ill. She died of lung cancer in 2007. I began to doubt if The Bigger Game was a worthy model and philosophy. I put the concept aside for a time and focused on other programs, but in the months that followed, one great leader at IBM, Alan Roe, kept calling. I had delivered a Bigger Game workshop to him and his peers in the New York area. Their team believed in the value of The Bigger Game. He thought I should keep building upon what Laura and I had created.

Although I had my fears and doubts, I kept seeing our concept transform the lives of those who played it. I accepted an invitation from Alan, a key leader of IBM's Australia group, to make a major international presentation for a select group of top performers from IBM's Asia-Pacific region. It marked my return to presenting The Bigger Game after Laura's death, and it proved to be a most fortuitous event. After my presentation, another innovative, forward-thinking IBM-er in the audience, Savoula Lidis, approached me with her own vision of a bigger game.

"I want more of this! My goal is to make people more conscious, responsible, and better leaders in our organization, so let's talk."

She offered to help me reach an even greater audience around the world. With her assistance over the last seven years, I have both championed and lived The Bigger Game on a global scale with IBM as a major player during that period. I was thrilled to bring my concept to IBM-ers around the world. And it really dovetailed with IBM's own bigger game of "Let's Build a Smarter Planet." Every time I see an IBM billboard with those words, I feel proud to have been a voice of support for their good work in our world. Thank you, IBM!

WHICH BRINGS ME TO YOU

This book offers guidance for applying The Bigger Game to daily life, whether in your personal development or your career—and quite possibly, in both.

This book is my way of taking your goodness to greatness. There are deeply spiritual aspects addressed in this book. Each of us is here for a reason. We were created to express a purpose, not just to survive, make a living, and then retire to our golden years.

The Bigger Game offers a philosophy and methodology for finding and releasing the full expression of your purpose and talents so that all of your years may be golden—and fun, too. Going back to when I was the leader of our church youth group, my off-the-wall decision to up the game and create a mission to Appalachia set in motion things I never anticipated. The same will happen to you.

Keep in mind that goals are overrated. It's fine to have them. I recommend them. But we have become so goal oriented in our work and personal lives that we aren't open to the magic and spontaneous opportunities that pop up. Go with your goals—love them and embrace them—but put more focus on the game you are playing, and watch yourself reach your goals magically.

The Bigger Game sets you free to live in a state of full engagement and creative play. What could be better than that? Are you ready? Let's begin!

Game on!

● ✖ ●

THE BIGGER GAME IS GOOD BUSINESS

Your bigger game can spring from anything you are involved in, whether it's working on a college degree, building a corporate career, starting a business, nurturing a family, or fighting for a cause. Some bigger games you may choose; some may choose you.

Many bigger games are played within the business environment, but no bigger games are business as usual. To qualify as bigger games, they must go above and beyond the norm. Often, they exceed the expectations of even their creators.

In this book's introduction, I cited two notable bigger game players, Melissa O'Mara and Alice Coles, and I promised to share their stories with you. This chapter is Melissa's home, because she has played her bigger games within major corporations, where she has been a top-level manager and in-house entrepreneur.

After she attended her first workshop for The Bigger Game, Melissa was inspired to make a move within her then employer, IBM, even though she wasn't at all sure where she was headed. She wanted to be in a more creative, free-flowing environment, and she felt compelled to have a bigger impact beyond her own direct reports in sales.

She transferred from the sales division to corporate coaching and leadership development at IBM. In effect, she was "enrolled" to be an ally in a bigger game that was already in progress at IBM, to inspire and enable a new style of leadership within the company's sales organizations, which was the game that had brought me and my workshops to IBM in the first place.

Melissa found that work more compelling, but she was still searching for her bigger game when IBM executives first explored global-sustainability issues within the corporation. The green movement within IBM captured her imagination.

"As individuals, we can change to more-efficient lightbulbs, sort our paper and plastics, and pledge to drive and fly less, but major corporations can have a much bigger impact by changing how they manufacture, ship, and dispose of their products at the end of their useful lives," she said.

Melissa came to see IBM and other major corporations as "global-change agents" for creating a sustainable future for people around the world. She joined a group of similarly inspired IBM employees who dubbed themselves "The Green Army" within Big Blue (a nickname for IBM). In her next series of moves, Melissa became, first, an innovation leader at IBM, and then smart-building business-development executive. Her compelling purpose was to accelerate the sustainability movement within IBM and corporate America.

At the same time that Big Blue was joining the green movement, it developed the Smarter Planets brand, which has been wildly successful in using modern technology and data analytics to take on the biggest challenges faced by clients around the world, including traffic congestion, pollution, food contamination, and crop disease.

IBM has concluded that business and institution leaders "have a unique opportunity to transform the way the world works" because of global integration and our "hyperconnected world." The Smarter Planet mission is to infuse intelligence into systems, processes, and infrastructures. IBM cites as examples Stockholm's use of smarter traffic systems to cut gridlock, reduce emissions, and increase public transportation; food-industry systems that use new technology to trace meat and poultry from the farm to store shelves; and smart health-care systems that dramatically lower costs.

Building a smarter planet is a bigger game that dramatically expanded the market for Big Blue while enhancing its profits. As her corporation spread its wings, Melissa did the same. While at IBM, she launched the Green Sigma Coalition, a network of nine leading energy and sustainability solutions providers—including IBM, Schneider Electric, Siemens, Cisco, and Johnson Controls, some of whom were direct competitors with each other—who committed to work together to accelerate the move toward enterprise sustainability.

Her work in that arena led Melissa to make an even greater leap in 2010. She left IBM to join Schneider Electric, a global energy-management company with annual sales of more than $29 billion and more than 130,000 employees worldwide.

IBM had been collaborating with Schneider in the Green Sigma Coalition. The energy-management company wanted to become more deeply involved in the green-building market, so company leadership offered Melissa the opportunity to lead Schneider's entire Green Buildings solutions initiative, a tremendous platform for her own bigger game.

Melissa's title at Schneider was most recently Chief Catalyst, Collaborative Innovation, U.S. Smart Cities.

She is responsible for launching Smart City innovation teams for selected U.S. cities and for enabling collaborative innovation across the Smart City value chain. Her mission is to maximize institutional and cultural response to environmental and economic challenges through smarter innovative solutions, cross-enterprise collaboration, and collective leadership. This is a Bigger Game that can and will have a dramatic impact on our lives.

BIGGER GAMES ARE SERIOUS BUSINESS

Our bigger games arise from who we are, and they determine who we become and what legacy we will leave. We create your bigger game by investing in it with the full force of who we are. In the process, we become thoroughly engaged and driven, not by goals or expectations but by our own compelling purpose.

This doesn't mean your bigger game has to be large in scope, although it often is. "Bigger" refers not to the size of the game but to the impact it has on you and your personal world around you. Like many who play bigger games, you may well discover leadership qualities you didn't know existed. You will feel more capable and more resilient, because playing your bigger game ignites your creativity and excites your mind.

One of the shifts that occurs when you play your bigger game, typically, is that you begin to think more like a leader. You'll find that your focus grows wider, encompassing not just yourself and others, but a much bigger, longer, and wider picture. That's the focus of a leader and a serious bigger game player.

Mats Lederhausen's father opened the first McDonald's in Sweden in 1973, and soon Mats was working under the golden arches, peeling potatoes and flipping burgers. His early fast-food experience put Mats on the fast track. He was running all of the McDonald's Sweden operations by the age of 35.

Despite his success with the giant fast-food chain, Mats didn't have a fast-food mentality. He led the corporation in embracing green practices before the environmental-sustainability movement had its own designated color. As early as 1995, his restaurants had programs for phasing out plastics, separating waste for recycling, buying organic, and aggressively conserving electricity. The thoughtful Swede also brought social consciousness to work, promoting nonviolence, integrating ethnic groups, and hiring workers with mental and physical disabilities.

Mats Lederhausen has never attended one of my workshops or seminars (as far as I know.) We've never met. Like many esteemed individuals I'll tell you about in this book, Mats is a natural bigger game player. The Bigger Game concepts I teach and extol are designed to help others understand what Mats Lederhausen and other naturals have somehow figured out for themselves and then put into action. They live the principles of The Bigger Game, and throughout this book, I'll point to them as role models and inspirations.

DEFINING MOMENTS

Lederhausen became a leader and visionary in his company, and then on a global scale, after discovering his compelling purpose and his own bigger game. What drove him?

He told one interviewer about coming to the realization while still in Sweden, "If tomorrow were the last day of my life, I wouldn't want to live it the way I was living." So he began to ask what he was meant to do. People he respected told him that he should remain in business and change the world from within, rather than dropping out, writing books, and giving lectures.

Then, a friend (and a great ally) asked Mats a simple question: "What would you do if you became CEO of McDonald's?"

Mats said he'd do corporate-wide what he'd done with the restaurants in Sweden. The friend suggested that Mats go to the McDonald's Oak Brook, Illinois, headquarters and share his ideas, noting that if they fired him or rejected his ideas, he could always leave the company.

Think of the defining moments in your life: were they triggered by a parent's comment, a teacher's praise, a coach's recognition, a friend's challenge, or a spark from within?

Whatever the source, look back on your defining moments and recall how you felt. Often your proud moments are accompanied by a sense of liberation and empowerment. You feel free to fully express who you are and what you believe in everything you do. That's how you feel when you discover a compelling bigger game.

After his friend encouraged Mats to take his philosophy and approaches to the leadership of McDonald's, he flew to Chicago and shared his vision with top executives. He told them that if they embraced his ideas, he would stay on with the company, but if they rejected them he would move on.

The McDonald's leadership responded by naming him global vice president for strategy. This was no small job. His promotion came at a time when the worldwide brand was struggling to reinvent itself in a changing market that was moving toward healthier food choices. In that environment, Mats likened his new role to that of a corporate psychiatrist/philosopher.

He looked to the corporation's past to create a vision for its future, noting that past successes provide the building blocks for what was to come. The key is to remain connected to your current customers while staying relevant to the constantly shifting marketplace. The strategy he devised was that McDonald's original premise of serving time-starved customers quality food was still valid, but its focus on continuous growth by adding stores was not. Instead of "growth by quantity," he advocated "growth by quality."

He realized that growth must be "deserved" in order to be sustainable, so as long as you are getting better, it's good to get bigger. However, if getting bigger hurts the quality of your goods or service, then it's a slippery slope.

SERVING A GREATER CAUSE

Bigger Games often serve a greater good, because the player experiences an expansion of perspective and a compelling desire to have a lasting impact. A writer, photographer, artist, or filmmaker may decide to focus on a subject that ignites a social movement. An athlete may decide to use her notoriety to serve as a spokesperson for a cause or a charity. A business leader may decide to make his company a force for social or political change.

Under Lederhausen's leadership, McDonald's worked to reduce and eventually eliminate trans-fatty acids as well as hormones and antibiotics in beef. Waste reduction and water purification were also tackled, as were work conditions in toy manufacturers in China. The underlying philosophy of the turnaround strategy devised by Mats was that companies should have "a purpose bigger than their product." That's also the compelling purpose of the company he left McDonald's to create. It's called BE-CAUSE, and it's focused on building companies on that foundational philosophy. His "ultimate dream" is to manage a set of businesses that are all born out of a purpose bigger than their products.

Mats is not an idealistic dreamer. A former member of the Swedish Marines Corps, he's a seasoned business veteran who rose to the highest levels of one of the world's most successful brands by putting his compelling purpose into action and achieving tangible results.

THE GAME OF GROWTH

Another important feature of your bigger games is that they require you to grow. In fact, if you already know how to do it, it's not a Bigger Game. But don't worry. Like Mats, you will be so compelled that you will find a way—and amazingly, you'll have no sense of struggling or frustration, only that liberating feeling that comes with expressing the full power of all of your gifts. In that state of being, you'll experience another phenomenon. You'll attract allies and supporters into your life like never before. Their complementary skills, talents, and knowledge will meld with yours. A team will form, sometimes without conscious effort, and you'll accomplish more than you ever could have done alone. Mats has noted this in his business experiences.

"My greatest sense of spirituality or connectedness is when I'm with people who come together for a cause much larger than themselves and do great work," he wrote in *EnlightenNext* magazine.

You may have had similar feelings. My own such experiences are the foundation of my belief that at our core, we are all Bigger Game players. Many of us are simply looking to find what our bigger games might be.

Mats has applied his compelling purpose to the international business world in the belief that more stakeholders (customers, employees, shareholders, and the larger community) want their businesses to think, act, feel, and be connected with a larger context. He calls this "spirituality in action."

THE GAME VS. THE GOAL

One of the biggest hurdles corporate employees have in embracing The Bigger Game is what I call "goal fixation." That's understandable, because their careers often depend upon hitting the numbers.

As I've mentioned, goals have a useful purpose in life and in business—no doubt about that. Yet, sometimes our fixation on goals (a deep-rooted comfort zone, by the way) narrows our vision to the point that we miss out on the larger context. In the case of the McDonald's fast-food empire, the focus on building more and more stores in a drive for sheer numbers proved to be a dangerous long-term goal because of its narrow focus.

In pursuing his personal bigger game, Lederhausen led McDonald's to its own bigger game, based on "growth by quality." This global brand still has goals, but the entire corporation is driven by a greater purpose, a compelling purpose.

This is not a new concept, by the way. And it's not the product of "soft" thinking or touchy-feely philosophy. The late management expert Peter Drucker wrote in his classic, *The Practice of Management*, published in 1954:

"If we want to know what a business is, we have to start with its *purpose.* And its purpose must lie outside of the business itself. In fact, it must be in society since a business enterprise is an organ of society. . . . Profit is not the explanation, cause, or rationale of business behavior and business decisions, but the test of their validity."

In our quest for profits today, we have unwillingly and unconsciously lost our way with this thinking. The Bigger Game was born out of a desire to return to this powerful concept. Okay, loosen the collar on your business shirt or blouse, and look at the personal dimension of that same philosophy. This quote is from another person who could hardly be considered a lightweight, Viktor Frankl, author of the classic *Man's Search for Meaning:*

"Don't aim at success—the more you aim at it and make it a target, the more you are going to miss it. For success, like happiness, cannot be pursued; it must ensue, and it only does so as the unintended side effect of one's dedication to a cause greater than oneself."

THE SHIFT

Once you play The Bigger Game and find your version of it personally or professionally, you create a huge paradigm shift. The entire focus shifts from the narrow (hitting the numbers) to a much larger context (growth through quality). When that happens, you enter a state of flow, much as my youth group did when we unwittingly found our bigger game, the mission trip to Annville.

When the paradigm shift occurs, creativity and innovation are sparked. You and your work teams don't get stuck on *how*. Instead, you innovate and create solutions as a natural result of the positive energy and excitement generated by your compelling purpose.

As a corporate coach and trainer, I've often been asked by CEO's and presidents to help their top managers and teams become more innovative, collaborative, and engaged. But you can't force people to innovate, collaborate, and be engaged by simply setting goals. You have to create an environment where these things are the natural result of a creative process. So, that's what I do. I create that environment by sending my clients off in pursuit of their bigger games *within* the organization.

While working with teams inside organizations around the globe, I often hear a common theme. People say they want to do their best and generate positive outcomes for their employers, and they also want to feel fulfilled by what they do. I've yet to meet a corporate employee or organization staff member who strives to do the worst-possible job. Yet, often corporations and organizations put good people in the wrong positions, or they place unreasonable pressure on them by demanding outcomes that are beyond their capabilities. What I see mostly is many who are not motivated simply because they are not compelled. Millions of dollars are spent each year on "leadership development." I daresay it's high time to focus on "bigger game development."

I get the sense that many businesses, government agencies, and nonprofits are frying in their own oils because of this focus on outcomes. Time after time, participants in my workshops and seminars tell me privately about their frustrations and anxieties because of intense pressures to meet quotas or goals that take all of the joy and creativity out of their jobs. Often they say they're planning to quit. I cringe at that, because employers and managers don't bring me in to inspire an employee exodus.

The Bigger Game can be an incredible tool for reinvigorating individuals and entire workforces. Lack of engagement by employees in their jobs costs companies and nonprofits billions of dollars each year. My goal in delivering Bigger Game workshops and seminars in the workplace is to close the gap between what employees desire to create and what the organization needs to grow.

There are always tasks that have to be accomplished. Goals have to be met. Inventories must be taken. Change must be implemented. They don't have to be mind-numbing and backbreaking experiences. This tool helps provide fresh perspectives that ignite creativity.

Innovation is nurtured in that sort of environment. You don't train people to be innovative. You create a space to nurture innovation, just as the nursery owner creates a greenhouse for the plants. That's what The Bigger Game model does. It creates a new context and environment in which innovation takes place and employees become more engaged and excited.

When the focus is on fostering creativity instead of hitting the numbers, amazing things can happen. Speaker Barbara Glanz often shares a story that exemplifies this. She'd been hired to lead a customer-service initiative for a grocery chain. She encouraged employees to create positive experiences and good memories for their customers so they'd want to come back to their stores. No quotas were set, no goals drawn up. Instead, with just a few simple words, an environment for innovation was created.

A 19-year-old grocery-store bagger named Johnny responded by creating his own bigger game. You may have seen a video about him on YouTube. Johnny called Barbara Glanz a month or so after her presentation. He first told her that he had Down syndrome and that her speech, at first, left him wondering what he could do in response to her call to create memories for customers, for he was simply a bagger. But then he had an inspiration.

After work each night, Johnny worked to come up with an inspiring "Thought for the Day." Sometimes he found them, and sometimes he made them up. Then his father helped him print out the thoughts on multiple slips of paper. Johnny took them to work each day. He then slipped one "Thought for the Day" in the bag of each customer he served before saying, "Thanks for shopping with us."

After Johnny had been doing this a few weeks, his store manager reported one day that he noticed the innovative bagger's checkout line was three times longer than any other. The manager quickly called for more cashiers to open more lanes, but none of the people in Johnny's line budged. They preferred to wait for Johnny and his "Thought for the Day" slips.

One customer told the manager that she'd started coming in the store whenever she was nearby, just as an excuse to receive one of Johnny's inspiring messages. The store manager later told Barbara that Johnny's efforts, his bigger game, had transformed the store, because he'd inspired other employees to find their own ways of reaching out to customers. The floral department, for instance, began saving its broken flowers and pinning them on customers as gifts.

Now Johnny had never participated in one of my workshops or seminars, but he proved himself a natural bigger game player. Johnny stepped out of his *comfort zone* of business as usual after hearing Barbara's presentation and developing a *hunger* for something more. He felt a *compelling purpose* to create an enhanced experience for his customers. Then, Johnny *assessed* his situation, wondering what he could do as just a bagger. He came up with his "Thought for the Day" slips and took a *bold action*—something above and beyond his usual duties. He recruited his father as an *ally* to help him make the slips, *investing* time and effort. Johnny's path can clearly be traced on The Bigger Game Board. I'll share more on the board with you in the next chapter.

Once again, this concept isn't necessarily about *big* or flashy undertakings; it's about feeding your hunger to fulfill a compelling purpose and do whatever it is that you're passionate about and driven to do because it excites and fulfills you. Your bigger game also can be played out within your current place of employment, as was the case with Johnny and Mats Lederhausen. It's also worth noting that these natural bigger game players led innovative and creative projects that also enhanced the outcomes for their employers.

WORKING TOGETHER

Often, I'll go into a big corporation to conduct a workshop and encounter employees who have workshop burnout. They all roll their eyes at the thought of another off-site workshop, "team-building" exercise, or "innovation" therapy session.

They've built boats together. They've walked on hot coals. They've sung Kumbaya around the corporate campfire. Everyone might feel good, and yet, they return to the office, where the boss wants to know if they'll hit their goals for the quarter. Business as usual is knocking at their door. That's to be expected, because shifting a paradigm is no small deal. It takes courage, conviction, and strong leadership. I've said in many a workshop, "Playing The Bigger Game is not for the faint of heart."

You can't fix a no-collaboration business team by putting it through a collaboration workshop. But you can fix it with my playful tool, because collaboration is a natural part of playing. Telling your sales team that profits must be doubled next year is a bigger goal but not a bigger game. Yet, a bigger game often leads to the accomplishment of bigger goals, because it springs from a compelling purpose and a hunger for something greater and more fulfilling.

If you or your organization focuses exclusively on outcomes and goals, then there's little energy left for creativity and innovation. If, instead, the focus is on doing what matters, genius is ignited. The result of igniting genius, by the way, very often means financial success for individuals and corporations. It's a safe bet, for example, that Mats Lederhausen didn't take a pay cut to become global vice president for strategy at McDonald's.

DEFAULT THINKING

Often, when I talk about focusing on purpose rather than goals, top corporate executives jump on the concept. For many of them, it's a reminder; it's not a new idea, yet it gets lost in the day-to-day grind of execution and results-oriented thinking. It's as if a light goes on. They love it at first. Then they slide back into their default mode: "But we still need to grow profits. How are we going to do that?"

My role is to help them make that paradigm shift, to think in fresh ways and to inspire them that there are profits at the end of the rainbow. As I nudge them toward their bigger games, they tense up and have trouble breathing. So, I say a magic word:

Apple.

When Apple's co-founder the late Steve Jobs stepped down from daily leadership and the organization brought in a new CEO from Pepsi, the leadership focus shifted to hitting the numbers. Profits, not innovation, became the primary goal, and the mighty brand that Jobs had created lost its way.

Meanwhile, after being booted out of his own company, Jobs licked his wounds for a while and then took his passion for innovation and creativity to Pixar Animation Studios and NeXT, which he revived as a major entertainment company. He sold Pixar to Disney and NeXT to Apple before returning as CEO to Apple, which was in great need of rejuvenation.

Jobs shifted the focus of Apple from simply manufacturing personal computers and laptops to serving as an entertainment company that seeks to delight its customers with innovative and beautifully designed products. "That's what a lot of customers pay us to do . . . to try to make the best products we can," he said. "And if we succeed, they'll buy them. And if we don't, they won't. And it'll all work itself out."

The result of Steve Jobs's shift to a bigger game is one of the greatest turnarounds in business history, and it started during a recession. It was driven by a hard-nosed businessman whom some have described as a tyrant. But you can't argue that Jobs lacked passion. He was driven to make products that customers love, which instills a culture of creativity and innovation. He focused less on Apple's being a computer company and more on its becoming an entertainment company with products such as iTunes and iPods at first, and then the iPhone. We all know how *that* worked out! And now Apple sells more computers than ever before. This new bigger game oriented toward entertainment even resulted in a name change of the company from Apple Computer, Inc., simply to Apple, Inc.—a game changer for sure.

Another advocate of this purpose-driven approach to business is John Mackey, who grew a tiny natural-foods store into an $8 billion retail chain called Whole Foods Market. Mackey's version of a bigger game is called Conscious Capitalism, which he believes will become the dominant paradigm of business in the 21st century.

Mackey believes corporations must refocus on purpose over profit by first serving stakeholders that include employees, customers, shareholders, suppliers, the community, and the environment. He maintains that when the welfare of stakeholders is made a priority in every business decision, they will flourish, the business will flourish, and the bottom line will flourish.

As part of this bigger game, Mackey stages Conscious Capitalism Summits in the United States, Europe, and India. He built Conscious Capitalism Alliance and created an audio series to get the message out and inspire other young entrepreneurs to be conscious capitalists. His purpose is to convince business leaders to focus on making a positive difference in the world in ways that result in higher profits and higher returns, too.

Mackey is a disciple of free-market capitalists Milton Friedman and Ayn Rand. He believes voluntary cooperation and spontaneous order can be channeled through free markets to the betterment of humanity. In his Bigger Game, self-interest and altruism can coexist and thrive simultaneously. Mackey told *Time* magazine, "One of the things that I'm trying to philosophically just destroy is this bifurcation that human beings are either greedy, selfish, only in it for themselves—or they're saints." (I'm not advocating a particular political viewpoint here, but rather simply underlying how clear John Mackey's compelling purpose is and how it has informed his Whole Foods bigger game.)

Like many natural-born bigger game players, Mackey aimed to do well by doing good, and by his own measure, he and Whole Foods are fulfilling that purpose by helping customers eat healthier foods, providing employees with a great place to work, allowing suppliers to grow and flourish with his business, and rewarding investors for their faith in his company.

The nation's largest seller of natural and organic foods, Whole Foods is unique in that regular employees hold 96 percent of the company's stock options, 5 percent of its after-tax profits go to charity each year, no executive can make more than 19 times the salary of the average employee, and no meat is purchased from factory farms. These are Bigger Game decisions indeed.

BIGGER GAMES INSPIRE COLLABORATION AND CREATIVITY

Leaders with a compelling purpose, like Mackey, often collaborate with others who are striving to up their games. Jeffrey Hollender was CEO of Seventh Generation, a natural-cleaning-products company, when Whole Foods began its expansion into big stores and needed products that aligned with its purpose. Hollender's purpose in co-founding this company was to change the cleaning-products industry by moving it away from toxic and wasteful ingredients to those more in tune with the environment.

Hollender's company has struggled financially because of Hollender's high standards for its products. To help bring financial health and his altruistic mission into harmony, Hollender has certified his company as a *B corporation,* a new category of for-profit corporate status requiring companies to consider factors other than earnings in their decision making. A B corporation company's board must consider environmental and social factors every time it makes a decision, and it's required to hit specific social and environmental performance targets.

My purpose-driven game back at Old Paramus Reformed Church inspired creativity and teamwork. I had a couple of dozen teenagers with little to no attention spans to wrangle into a collaborative team for my ambitious youth-group mission to the Appalachians. I didn't know how to make them collaborate or innovate or engage, but I didn't have to. They just did. We'd never held a 24-hour dance marathon, but we pulled it off as part of our bigger game.

Innovation was an outcome. Collaboration was an outcome. Engagement was an outcome.

My youth-group members were compelled to be innovative, collaborative, and engaged, because we were all working toward a greater purpose. They were like the mother who somehow finds the strength to lift her car to free the child trapped beneath a rear wheel, or the passing stranger who breaks through a locked door and saves the elderly woman from a burning building as it collapses around him. Compelled people do amazing things.

● ✖ ●

CHAPTER

3

ON THE BOARD
AND IN THE GAME

Upon first stepping up to The Bigger Game Board, my clients and workshop participants typically say, "Where do I start?"

The answer is, "Anywhere you want."

I must warn you as I warn them: once you step onto The Bigger Game Board, you'll never want to leave. The good news is that you can stay on the board, at least figuratively, for the rest of your life. That's a key point, by the way. When I give my workshops and seminars around the world, I take a king-size version of The Bigger Game Board with me. During the course of my presentations, I place the game board and all of its squares on the floor. Then I have participants physically step onto each square as we explore the concepts behind it.

I also give people their own smaller version of The Bigger Game Board, about the same size of this book, so they can always have it with them. But the most important version of the board is the one implanted in their minds. Once you've picked up the concept for playing, you begin to live it, and the game board starts to live within your head and heart.

I've seen this happen countless times. The names of the squares provide a means for expressing where you stand at virtually any point in your life. Notice that they're called *squares,* by the way, not *boxes.* The word *box* conjures up a limiting image, which is not their intention. The squares themselves are each like the "current location" indicator on a GPS map. Mentally, you can always determine where you are in your quest for meaning and fulfillment just by summoning up the image of the board and its individual squares.

I've found that people come to understand the game and the squares on the board more quickly if I present them in the order they're presented in this book, which is also the order I present them in my Bigger Game workshop. This is because you can start anywhere on the game board, like in tic-tac-toe; however, as you play you will pick up on a strategy, just as you do with tic-tac-toe.

I'll go into each square in more depth later, but for now, here's a quick description of the individual squares on The Bigger Game Board:

Hunger. This is the square you occupy when you feel a powerful desire for something more—even if you have no idea what that something is. Here is where you can begin to think about what you're hungering for and what the world hungers for that you could provide.

Compelling Purpose. You stand on this square when you have defined or are looking for a purpose that inspires and drives you. Usually this is something you would do for free, because the payoff is so perfectly matched to your needs and desires.

Comfort Zones. This is the square you occupy when you feel comfortable, complacent, or somewhere in between—although being in a comfort zone can also be uncomfortable. If being in a comfort zone fulfills, excites, and ultimately serves you, that's fine and dandy. Stay right there. But if you find yourself staying in a comfort zone because you're afraid to leave it for something better, for whatever reason, then you should look for another place on the board and in your life. Comfort zones, in this model, are neither good nor bad. The question to ask in the Comfort Zone square is, "Does this comfort zone serve me well or not?"

Gulp. This is the high-energy square. This is the place where excitement and fear feel like one and the same. When you're considering a bold action and your palms are sweaty and your mouth dry, you take a position on this square so that you know it's perfectly normal and not at all bad to feel exactly how you're feeling. Then, you turn all that potentially negative energy into a positive force for change.

Investment. This is the deposit box. Here, you consider, plan, and process the investments of time, money, talent, blood, sweat, and tears that you'll need to make in order to create, run, and sustain your bigger game.

Allies. Consider this the friends and family square and then some. Mostly this is where you stand when you're recruiting, building, and nurturing the support network for you and your bigger game.

Sustainability. This is another checkup stop. Here, you think about what you need to do to sustain yourself and your bigger game so that both of you can have a lasting impact.

Assess. Head for this square when you feel the need to ask, "How am I doing? Where am I, and where do I want to go?"

Bold Action. This square is at the center of the board, because playing your bigger game will, sooner or later, require a bold move. When you reach that point, whether you're ready or not, this is where you go to make the leap.

NAVIGATING THE GAME BOARD

The game-board design is similar to those of tic-tac-toe or Twister. There's no required starting point in either of those games, just as there's none in this one. You can begin on any square. All squares are of equal weight and value, but feel free to have your favorites. Once you've become adept at using the game board, you may even want to add your own unique squares. Go nuts! (It's your game, after all.)

Often when clients can't decide where to begin, I'll ask, "Where are you in your life right now?" Then they ponder the choices on the game board. Are they . . .

✖   . . . in a *comfort zone?*

✖   . . . *hungry* for something more, yet don't know what it is?

✖   . . . driven by a *compelling purpose* or longing to find one?

✖   . . . *assessing* their lives or careers?

✖   . . . ready to take *bold action?*

✖   . . . feeling thrilled and a bit nervous, and having a *Gulp* moment?

✳   . . . wondering how to create *sustainability* for your dream?

✳   . . . lining up a support team of *allies?*

✳   . . . considering or making an *investment* of time, money, and talent?

STUCK NO MORE

Whatever your emotional, mental, or physical state, you're always on the board somewhere. Once you've located where you are, then you can decide what your next move should be. You'll never be without somewhere to go.

Ruth was struggling in her corporate job, when she attended one of my workshops. She said she felt "stuck." That's a very common feeling. I brought out The Bigger Game Board, gave her a nine-minute tutorial, and then told her she'd never be stuck again.

"With this, you always can identify where you are," I said. "So from there, you can figure out where you want to go next."

The game board is designed to provide both insight and information. You may already have the insight and information you need, but playing The Bigger Game helps draw it out of you. About ten minutes into Ruth's first visit to the game board, she burst into tears. She realized that she really wasn't stuck in her job and her life after stepping onto the Assess square for just a few minutes. There, she took a quiet moment to examine what was in her heart and came to a realization: she'd only felt stuck because there was a compelling purpose crying out to be served.

Ruth considered all of the problems she'd been having at work and in her relationships, and concluded that they all stemmed from the fact that what she really wanted to be doing was very different from the path she was on. Simply moving to the Compelling Purpose square gave her the permission and courage to recognize and acknowledge this disparity and incongruence in her life. After that, it was "game on" for Ruth.

Once she'd accepted her compelling purpose, Ruth moved on to the Allies square, because she wanted to share it with her boss, one of those rare leaders who's a champion and encourager for her team members. She wanted her employees to be in jobs that compelled and fulfilled them whenever possible, because they performed at their highest levels in those jobs.

Ruth stayed with her employer, a global company, but she took a different position that allowed her to apply her talents and knowledge toward her compelling purpose. In other words, she went from being in a comfort zone where she felt stuck to doing work that really mattered to her and excited her.

I can't tell you too much about exactly what she's doing due to confidentiality, but Ruth, whose daughter had a bad experience in a hospital, is working on a bigger game to revolutionize the national health care system from the inside out. Her company is a total ally in this game. It may even be large enough to deeply impact the current system of health care in her nation. Now that's a bigger game!

THE GAME THAT NEVER ENDS

Once you decide on which square to begin with, your next moves usually become obvious, even instinctive. Like tic-tac-toe or Twister, you can occupy several squares at once on The Bigger Game Board. That's about it as far as similarities go between this and any traditional board game, because you have no opponent or competition. Another unique feature is the fact that you never have to stop playing your own version.

Welcome to the game that never ends! The Bigger Game is a playful, easy, and fun coaching concept, but as most discover, playing it can change your life forever. I've had many individuals tell me this, but there are always skeptics and doubters. I once had a participant in a corporate workshop tell me straight up:

"This is the most simplistic and silly concept I've ever heard of!"

I didn't disagree, but I told him that the "game" concept is designed to provide a simple, common language and to activate clarity and understanding for the players. That same skeptic returned the next day and said he'd used The Bigger Game Board with his family and ignited a very meaningful conversation.

I told him, "That's the purpose: to launch a conversation about how you intend to create the life you long to live."

Talk about an *aha!* moment. He was on board with The Bigger Game from that moment on.

We often hear that life is a game, so I've given you a game board to live with. If the concept of a game board is too retro as a metaphor for you, try thinking of this board as your basic operating system, similar to those used on your desktop or laptop computer. While you're on your computer, the operating system hums along quietly, always there, helping you do what you need to do.

The game board works the same way. While you're playing whatever bigger game you want, the game board is always there to support you in whatever you want to do. All that's required to begin play is an earnest desire to have a more meaningful and successful life and conscious awareness of where you are right now, where you want to be, and where you need to go to get there.

BIGGER GAME BOARD (BGB) STRATEGY

The Bigger Game Board is a constant reference point, an inspirational launchpad, and a check-in station for players pursuing their passions. It's all about getting out of the stands and onto the playing field of life. In the stands, you can drink overpriced warm beer, eat sodium-packed hot dogs, cheer, scream, yell, and pretend to be the quarterback. On the field, you'll use every bit of your strength, wisdom, courage, passion, and creative energy to actually be the star of the game. In the stands, you watch history in the making. On the field, you make history to inspire others to want to play as well.

To play your bigger game, you have to be on the field of life, and The Bigger Game Board serves as a metaphor for that. Whether you stand on it physically or just imagine yourself moving from square to square, when you're on the game board, you become engaged and driven by your compelling purpose. One of my workshop participants said the concept reminds her of a favorite bumper sticker: "The people who change the world are the ones who show up." In other words, to be a game changer, you have to be *in* the game—not in the stands watching.

So often, people who come to my seminars and workshops have the sense that they want something more, but they have no idea or only a vague concept of what that is. Then, when they step into The Bigger Game concept by taking a position on the game board, something clicks—maybe not right away, but usually it doesn't take long. You may have to be more daring than ever before. You must decide to set something in motion even without knowing what it is. It's like stepping into a mystery. Another player in training said that beginning a bigger game session is a little like starting a pregnancy: you know something is coming that will change your life; you just don't know exactly what form it will take.

You may find that giving up the "need to know" will take a huge weight off your shoulders and your mind. Zen masters describe this as "being in the now." Giving up the need to know also frees you up to improvise as you go, which is an essential freedom in today's world. Improvisation is a key to self-expression, which is a critical aspect of the human condition. We all want to express ourselves, whether it's through our work, our creativity, our children, or the objects that adorn our lives.

NAMING YOUR GAME

Your unique bigger game lies at the intersection of what your heart desires and what the world needs. It's an inside-out process: going within yourself, finding what compels you, and then taking it out to find its place in the universe.

This is matchmaking to a great degree, and one of my favorite matches was found by my client Bob Pranga, who hired me as his coach in 1993 because he was feeling lost. He'd been struggling to make it as an actor while working three jobs as a waiter, tour guide, and department-store clerk. Even with three jobs, he was $60,000 in debt.

We talked once a week for a year, focusing on his passions, his priorities, and the mark he hoped to make on the world. In our discussions, Bob kept coming back to one particular interest, and every time he talked about it, his eyes lit up. While working for Macy's, the famed department store in Manhattan, Bob had decorated the huge Christmas tree, which is an annual tradition and big attraction for the store. He decorated the tree so beautifully that many people complimented him, including the actress Mia Farrow.

Bob mentioned this several times during our first few discussions. Then one day, he added, "I love decorating for Christmas so much that I've even wondered if I could make a living at it."

My Bigger Game alert immediately went off. "Why don't you do that?" I asked. I explained to Bob that starting his own Christmas-decorating business matched up well with his desire for the freedom to set his own hours and workload. "You love Christmas, and you love being independent; why not organize your life around those two loves?"

Within a year, Bob had established a brand as Dr. Christmas, tree stylist to the stars. He found a great ally by attracting a good friend, Debi Staron. Their skillful decorating and engaging personalities attracted a clientele that included Ryan Seacrest, Paris Hilton, the Jonas Brothers, Kate Hudson, Whoopi Goldberg, Heidi Klum, and Leeza Gibbons.

His business has grown to also providing holiday decorations for movies and television shows such as *Nip/Tuck, American Horror Story, Chuck, Veronica's Closet,* as well as the Home Shopping Network. Dr. Christmas also decorates for a corporate clientele that includes Walgreens, Walmart, Tiffany & Co., The Beverly Hilton, Macy's Herald Square, I. Magnin, The Walt Disney Studios, MGM, Warner Bros., and Paramount Pictures.

Like Bob Pranga, you may need help unlocking the keys to your future and your fulfillment. Chances are you aren't broken. You don't need to be fixed. You're just stuck. Like Bob's alter ego, Dr. Christmas, I know you have all you need to create the life of your dreams. The Bigger Game is designed to help you find your way there.

Michelangelo believed that within each piece of marble was a sculpture waiting to be revealed. He felt his role was to chip away the outer rock to reveal the beauty within. That's the perspective that went into creating The Bigger Game. You may feel stuck because you have been focused on what you're lacking, but when you play on the game board, you focus on your gifts and how to unleash their beauty and power.

Your bigger game emerges when you tap your creativity and find your true purpose. When you plug into that powerful dynamic, your energy level soars and everybody wins: you, your business, and those who care about you and work with you.

Think of a proud moment in your life, a time when you surprised yourself by accomplishing something special. Now reflect on that accomplishment and the impact it had on you. Did thinking about that proud moment boost your confidence? Did you become more open to opportunities? Are you a different person today as the result of that accomplishment?

If you answered yes to those questions, then congratulations, you're already a bigger game player! We all have the ability to do amazing things and have a positive impact. The Bigger Game is simply a tool for tapping into your inherent abilities by opening your eyes, focusing your mind, and unleashing your talents—and the board is where you go to free yourself from whatever limitations may have been imposed on you, either by yourself or by others.

So let's look at each of the squares in greater depth, shall we? As I mentioned earlier, I will explain the squares in the same order that I do in my Bigger Game workshops. I begin with the Hunger square, because hunger is what drives you to seek a bigger game in the first place. And I then jump around in describing subsequent squares, which is a reflection of the fact that when you play on The Bigger Game Board, you, too, will find that you can start anywhere and move about freely according to the flow of your own game.

● ✖ ●

PART II

GET
IN THE
GAME

CHAPTER 4

HUNGERING FOR SOMETHING MORE

Have you ever found yourself standing in front of your refrigerator with the door open while thinking, *I'm hungry. I just don't know what I want?*

The Hunger square on The Bigger Game Board is the place you want to be when you feel that same sort of craving for "something more" in your life but aren't exactly sure what that *something* might be. It sits next to the Comfort Zone square, because when we are in a comfort zone for too long, we naturally become hungry for something more. Boredom is a sign of too much comfort-zone living, which in turn then activates hunger for something new, different, or better.

Theologian Frederick Buechner wrote, "The place God calls you to is the place where your deep gladness and the world's deep hunger meet." The Bigger Game Board is a tool for figuring out just what will bring that "deep gladness" into your life and where you can unleash it.

You step onto the game board's Hunger square to acknowledge a hunger in your spirit, just as you step in front of the refrigerator because of hunger pangs in your belly. Okay, so you get the concept: The world is your fridge! Anyone want to break for a snack?

Maybe the hunger in your spirit is triggered by boredom and a desire for something more challenging, or the sense that you want to make a bigger contribution at work or in the world. Maybe your hunger is for something more in your personal life. Whatever the yearning, consider it a good thing. It means you have hope and are open to possibilities and opportunities. All of these are components for a vital and meaningful life. So be glad when you step onto the Hunger square. Once you're standing in front of life's Frigidaire, your choices present themselves. You then can decide what will satisfy your hunger and go after it by playing your bigger game.

When you step onto the Hunger square, either physically or in your mind's eye, your first thoughts should be, *What do I really want? What puts a fire in my belly? What's missing? What would fulfill me and give greater meaning to my life?*

Unleash that hunger. Gorge yourself on the possibilities. Hunger is visceral and internal, and it's one of your vital signs. Feeling hungry means you are alive and well. We're hardwired to feel hunger and feed it. It's a survival tool. When you're starving for nourishment, you'll go to extraordinary measures. You might even eat worms or cockroaches or, in a worst-case scenario, *my* cooking! (Just kidding—I am actually a decent cook these days.)

The Bigger Game Board's Hunger square isn't about that sort of hunger, of course. But the desire for something more in our lives is every bit as powerful once we activate it. And when you feed that hunger, it's better than the greatest meal you've ever had. So why wouldn't you want to activate something so powerful within you? Why wouldn't you do something that fulfills you and gives richer meaning to your life?

Yet many people don't act on their yearning for better lives. Some ignore it or let it lie dormant because they're afraid to make a change, or they settle for less because the prospect of doing more seems like too much work or too complicated. But very often, our hunger is triggered by a change in perspective. Suddenly, we see things in a different way, through a different lens, and our hunger becomes activated to the point where we can no longer ignore it.

THREE TRIGGERS TO ACTIVATE HUNGER

I've observed three trigger points that activate hunger. There may be more, but let's look at the three I've defined, which are called as follows:

* ✖ "No, not that!"
* ✖ "What's missing?"
* ✖ "More of that!"

The first, "No, not that!" is a perspective shift that activates hunger when there's a change in the status quo, and it's often not a welcome change. Many a "NIMBY" (*not in my backyard*) lawsuit or protest has been triggered by a "No, not that!" awakening. One of the more powerful hunger activations I've ever heard of brought sweeping change to a community that had gone virtually unnoticed and uncared for over 300 years.

Hunger Trigger 1: "No, Not That!"

The second notable bigger game player I cited in the introduction, Alice Coles, is a natural bigger game player who rallied her neighbors and transformed the community they lived in. Her bigger game provides one of my favorite examples of one triggered by a "No, not that!" hunger activation.

Prior to the mid-1990s, very few of the 150 residents of the Bayview community in Virginia had running water in their humble homes. Most lived in rented tar-paper shacks without plumbing. They carried water from outdoor wells, which were often polluted by their outhouses. Fires were an even greater danger. At least 11 Bayview residents, 6 of them children, died in fires caused by faulty wiring or overturned oil lamps over a 25-year period.

Hidden away from the region's more affluent retirement and residential communities, the 300-year-old village had long been a neglected enclave. Many of the same families have lived there for generations. Most, including Alice Coles, are African-American descendants of slaves who were freed after the Civil War.

They took pride in their deep roots and in their close-knit community with its quiet, rural setting, but what little they had was rapidly dwindling. Most who worked had jobs in agriculture and the seafood industry, which have dried up in recent decades. As its residents became more and more destitute, their secluded village was all but forgotten.

Then in 1995, state officials selected a 270-acre site in the middle of Bayview for a new maximum-security prison. They thought it would bring jobs and commerce to the long-suffering area, but Alice Coles and other residents said, "No, not that!" This single mother of two, who earned just $5,000 a year as a crab picker, had long hungered for something more for her children and her community. But what she wanted was not a hulking prison dumped into the middle of her town. She and other opponents made that point very clear to state officials who had done little to help them in the past.

Coles and her cousin Cozzie Lockwood organized a grassroots campaign to fight the prison and push for an economic and residential redevelopment program in Bayview. When they began, they had no clue what they were doing other than standing in opposition to powerful leaders. But as Mark Twain said, "Hunger is the handmaid of genius."

The people of Bayview had suffered in silence for decades, but the thought of a maximum-security prison forced upon them awakened their outrage and hunger. The descendants of slaves weren't sure exactly what they wanted for their village, but they knew it wasn't a huge complex built to keep others in chains and behind bars.

The Bayview residents fighting the prison lined up allies, including the NAACP, tourism boosters, and environmentalists who worried about the prison's impact on the fragile coastal region. They won the fight against the prison in 1995. But their pleas for state officials to come up with more positive economic-development programs for their community went unheeded for nearly three years.

Finally, Bayview residents decided to act on their hunger. They feared that if they didn't take control of their own destinies, some other powerful forces would move onto the vacant prison site and build something even worse. After three years of pushing for change, the locals took bold action and formed Bayview Citizens for Social Justice to lobby for their own vision of a bigger game.

Coles, a leader by nature, not by training, schooled herself as an organizer and community activist at workshops and seminars. Then she and her neighbors rounded up allies to apply for government grants. They enlisted the help of neighboring community groups, as well as architects, environmentalists, the NAACP, and other advisors and organizations drawn to their cause.

When they won their first grants, they focused on pressing health and safety issues. They dug community wells and septic systems and then undertook a massive community cleanup that collected thousands of pounds of trash and demolished fire-damaged structures. Then, they began to rebuild and reinvigorate their community by creating a ten-acre communal farm and garden, from which they sold produce and plants.

Their small successes spawned dreams of an even bigger game: to take the land once designated for the prison and develop it as a new Bayview, featuring modern apartments, townhouses, and single-family homes along with a grocery, community technology center, greenhouse, and day-care center.

Coles and her team secured financing to buy the land with the help of a nonprofit, and then they applied for more government assistance for the new housing. They publicized the plight of the community in the media and drew support from politicians and government agencies. Over time, they lured more than $10 million in assistance from dozens of public and private sources.

Once the funding was lined up, Coles tapped the expertise of a veteran rural-poverty program manager, who handled the paperwork and construction coordination for the revitalization of Bayview, which continues to this day, following the plan set out by the residents themselves. Those plans have led to the construction of more than 40 subsidized rental units in the revitalized Bayview Rural Village. The development has more than 80 single- and multifamily residences, and it lies just across the street from the tar-paper shacks where residents lived before they undertook their inspiring bigger game.

A VISION FULFILLED

When state officials announced plans to put the maximum-security prison in impoverished Bayview, they didn't expect community opposition. After all, the prison would have brought hundreds of jobs and a stronger economy to the community. But Alice Coles and her community disagreed with the state's vision for her ancestral home. They wanted new jobs, new homes, and retail development, but she also wanted to preserve the town's rural character and small-town traditions.

Residents wanted to re-create Bayview according to their own vision, not that of outsiders. I love the fact that when it came time to design and build the new housing for her community, Coles insisted that each building should have a front porch because, "That's where our family life was spent." She won that fight, too. I can only imagine the *Gulp* moment when they had to say to the government that the deal was off unless front porches were put on their homes.

Coles and her neighbors had their hunger awakened by a "No, not that!" trigger. They wanted something more, a better life and a healthier, safer, and more-modern community. That strong hunger drove them to create a truly remarkable bigger game. As we move through the rest of the squares on The Bigger Game Board in the chapters that follow, you'll see that many of these topics also came into play in the revitalization of Bayview, Virginia.

For example, while it may seem strange at first, the maximum-security prison was actually an ally of Coles and other residents, because the threat of the prison drove them out of a comfort zone—they'd grown complacent despite the lack of creature comforts—giving them a compelling purpose and leading them to take bold action in opposing the prison proposed by powerful government officials, from whom they then enlisted help to modernize their village. I'm sure there were many major *Gulp* moments during this period, too.

The Sustainability square was another major factor in their bigger game. Bayview residents were determined to sustain and preserve the town's traditions while rebuilding and modernizing. They didn't feel that erecting a prison in their midst was the way to do that, so they focused on economic-development projects closer to those traditions.

Also, before they moved residents into the new housing, they conducted classes and workshops to help them with the transition to making monthly payments for electricity, water, and other services that were new to them as owners and renters of modern housing.

Moving into the new homes was a jarring experience, even for Coles, who led the way as she pursued her compelling purpose. She told one interviewer, "I never believed in this lifetime that I would actually live like people."

Throughout this process, which began in the mid-1990s and continues today, Coles and other residents have had to assess where they were and what they needed to do next. They also spent a great deal of time on the Investment square, putting long hours into planning and carrying out their mission.

Their bigger game has garnered national attention and praise. Coles and her allies from within and outside the community have been honored by government and private organizations, and featured in print media; television news shows, including *60 Minutes;* and a documentary. One of my favorite bits of wisdom from Alice Coles is her belief that just as "big doors hang on small hinges," one person can make a difference in this world.

"If I couldn't be the door that opened . . . to a better life, [I'd] be the hinge to hold the door," she said.

There's so much to admire about Bayview's bigger game. Perhaps most impressive is the residents' commitment to fighting the prison, and then, over more than a decade, they upped the game and dramatically improved their lives and the lives of their children and grandchildren. That incredible commitment replaced their longtime apathy and disengagement when the "No, not that!" call to action was triggered.

Hunger Trigger 2: "What's Missing?"

The "What's missing?" trigger for activating hunger usually comes with a realization that there's a need that has either been overlooked or underserved. The missing piece might be in your work, in your relationships or private life, or in the world around you. Sometimes, as in the case of Ibrahim Salih, our hunger is awakened by this trigger when we realize that others are missing something that we may have come to take for granted or have acquired and want others to have as well.

Nearly everyone who knows Ibrahim Salih talks about the deep gladness that radiates from him. It's not just his charismatic personality or his high-wattage smile. I'm definitely not impartial here, but I think the joy emanating from and around Ibrahim springs from the fact that he's a natural bigger game player.

My admittedly biased theory is supported by one obvious bit of circumstantial evidence: Everything about Ibrahim is big! He was a soccer star in his home village of Aboabo, Ghana, until the age of 12, when his coaches suggested that despite his athletic gifts, Ibrahim might better fit on an American basketball court. He took up the game and, four years later, was on his way to the United States, thanks to the 1 Dream Foundation, which helps low-income athletes from impoverished countries receive education in the United States.

Ibrahim stood six feet six inches in height by the time he left Ghana for America. He played basketball for two years at a Maryland high school before graduating and joining the basketball team at Hill College in Hillsboro, Texas, where he has become a top student, campus leader, and something of a hero to everyone he meets.

His former coach, Mark Berokoff, described him simply as "the greatest kid on this earth, with the best smile in the world."

"His dream is to be a professional in the NBA, but he will make his real mark in helping people and having them fall in love with him," the coach said. "Many people have had their lives changed just by being around him."

That's quite a testimonial from a coach about a player, but the more you learn about Ibrahim, the more impressive he appears. You might think that the opportunity to escape the poverty of his youth and to earn a college degree in the United States would be enough of a bigger game for this young man. Yet Ibrahim has a powerful hunger that goes far beyond elevating his own life.

On his return visits to his home village in Africa, Ibrahim was troubled by the disparity between the quality of life he enjoyed in the United States and that of the impoverished children in his home village. He felt a responsibility to do whatever he could to ease their burden, especially when it came to providing basic needs like food, water, and access to health care.

Driven by his desire to reach back and make a difference in his native village, Ibrahim followed his compelling purpose and took bold action. He raised funds in the United States and, at the age of 19, began a campaign to build a self-development center in Aboabo. The center provides basic food, health programs, and much-needed medical supplies, including diabetes-testing equipment, shoes, clothing, mosquito netting, hygiene training, and other goods and services.

Ibrahim plans on returning to Ghana after receiving his college degree. His goal is to help other young people access similar educational opportunities and further improve the quality of life in his homeland.

Ibrahim's desire to help others matched the needs in his African village, and the result was a bigger game that is changing his life and the lives of many others for the better. The deep gladness that people see in this young man is born of his hunger triggered by the realization that something was missing in the lives of his fellow villagers.

Hunger Trigger 3: "More of That!"

This trigger for activating hunger runs counter to the notion that you can have too much of a good thing. In some cases, more of a good thing is even better! At least that's what they taught me when I was training as a waiter at The Cheesecake Factory, home of heaping helpings. Okay, maybe too much cheesecake isn't a good thing for your waistline, but there are certain cases where more is better in business, in our personal lives, and in the greater world. For most companies, having more sales is a good thing. For most people, experiencing more loving relationships is always welcomed. And in the greater world, who would argue that we don't need more compassion, more support for those in need, and more helping hands for those in need?

As in the cases of many natural-born bigger game players, Brenda Eheart had a powerful hunger that, once activated, had many triggers. This pioneering sociologist's initial step into a bigger game came in the early 1990s. In her research at the University of Illinois at Urbana-Champaign, she'd done a ten-year study of young people who "age out" of the foster-care system after spending most of their lives bouncing from one foster home to the next. Most grew up never knowing what it was like to have a stable, loving family. Fewer than half even finished high school.

As you might imagine, Eheart, who has a daughter and an adopted son, found that a high percentage of these unfortunate individuals experienced many challenges as adults, including drug and alcohol addiction, depression, and criminal convictions. Unlike most academics, who simply report their findings and move on to the next study, Eheart couldn't do that. Motivated by a "No, not that!" trigger after her review of the failings of the foster-care system, she formed a group of others who were outraged by the inadequacies of the status quo.

After several years of pondering the problem and wondering how to remove more children at an early age from foster care and give them permanent homes and families, Eheart came up with a plan for what seemed like an impossible, utopian concept. She and her group conceived of a community of families dedicated to adopting children from foster care and raising them together in a mutual-support network.

The costs and logistics seemed impossible to manage until Eheart found a ready-made place: a shuttered former U.S. Air Force base in Rantoul, Illinois, with an abandoned neighborhood of officer's quarters along winding, tree-lined streets. With the help of a million-dollar state grant, that former base became Hope Meadows, a groundbreaking community with ten adoptive families—some single-parent, some two-parent—caring for former foster children who might otherwise never have known a permanent home.

Eheart, who had many allies in her effort, recruited and carefully screened adults who were willing to adopt and parent at least four children from foster care. In return for this, each adoptive family received a stipend and a free home on the former air base. Most of these homes were formerly officer's duplexes converted to six-bedroom single-family homes.

As her bigger game was coming together, the academic turned activist felt another hunger pang activated by the "What's missing?" trigger. While Eheart had planned for a network of child-welfare experts and therapists to be involved in Hope Meadows, she felt that there needed to be another, more intimate layer of support. Her work as a sociologist had also made Eheart aware that the strongest families were those with multiple generations present. So, she added another dimension to Hope Meadows, recruiting more than 40 senior citizens to move into subsidized apartments in the community in return for agreeing to volunteer as "foster grandparents" for the adopted children.

The seniors also derive a great deal from being part of the community, which allows them to feel needed and useful. Studies have shown that the social bonds they form naturally with the children and families have resulted in improved health for many of the foster grandparents. Several of them who'd been using walkers, or were sickly or generally inactive, have become rejuvenated and physically active because of their involvement in the community.

As of early 2013, Hope Meadows was home to 48 seniors, 36 children, and 14 parents. The children of this healing village have succeeded by every measure. Even though just 30 percent of foster children nationwide graduate from high school, the rate for Hope Meadows kids is 100 percent. Several have gone on to college, including one young lady who received a scholarship to Yale University after expressing her desire for an Ivy League education on an episode of *The Oprah Winfrey Show* that featured Hope Meadows residents.

From its founding in 1995, the five-block village of Hope Meadows has been a resounding success, with an adoption-success rate of nearly 90 percent. The intergenerational adoptive model has attracted grants, studies, and high praise from academics; civic, social, and philanthropic groups; and even the White House. The W. K. Kellogg and Heinz Foundations, along with other grant providers, have bought into the concept. In fact, Kellogg provided a $7.7 million grant to help Generations of Hope—which was created to replicate the Hope Meadows model in other areas—develop similar programs in 18 states.

You probably won't be surprised to learn that despite the great success of her bigger game and the many awards she has received as its creator, Eheart hungered for "More of that!" Many times, a "More of that" does come after a "No, not that!" or from "What's missing?" Sometimes, your bigger game can be about linking up with a successful preexisting bigger game simply because you are compelled by "More of that" in your world.

After winning the prestigious Heinz Award for the Human Condition in 2008, she used part of the $250,000 grant to create an even bigger game called Generations of Hope. The goal of this new bigger game is to replicate the success of Hope Meadows across the country and, if possible, around the world.

In fact, Eheart has inspired others to take her model for social change and run with it. Similar communities have already been built in Scottsdale, Arizona; Easthampton, Massachusetts; and Portland, Oregon. The Hope Meadows model has been adapted for New Life Village in Tampa, Florida, which will one day provide permanent adoptive homes for older children and sibling groups in foster care. In Charlottesville, Virginia, a group inspired by Hope Meadows is developing an intergenerational community to help single mothers who have been incarcerated for crimes to reenter life upon their release.

Another Hope Meadows offshoot in the works is Osprey Village, a residential community near Hilton Head, South Carolina, that serves mentally and developmentally disabled adults supported by senior volunteers and retirees. In New Orleans, a Hope Meadows–inspired support community called Bastion has been proposed to serve "wounded warriors" from Iraq and Afghanistan, veterans who have suffered severe traumatic brain injuries. They hope to house 155 residents one day on a former naval-support base.

The Bastion project is of particular interest to me, because it has received a $100,000 grant from the Bob Woodruff Foundation, which was created by my upstate New York neighbor Bob Woodruff, the ABC television correspondent who has recovered from his own traumatic brain injuries suffered while covering the Iraq War in 2006. I am always reminded how small the world becomes when one plays a bigger game. The amazing thing about these wonderful efforts is that, like Hope Meadows and Generations of Hope, they tend to inspire and spawn even more bigger games because their success activates hunger in other people who are yearning for something more.

THE HUNGER INSIDE

Laura Whitworth, my co-founder of The Bigger Game, used to say that far too many people live with their hunger dials turned down. That's not a problem for natural-born bigger game players who use their hunger to create lives that fulfill them. The spiritual writer Thomas Merton wrote, "If you want to identify me, ask me not where I live or what I like to eat or how I comb my hair, but ask me what I am living for, in detail, ask me what I think is keeping me from living fully for the thing I want to live for."

I've worked with clients who have purposely repressed or ignored their hunger pangs, because they were locked into a comfort zone that kept them from living fully. Others have admitted to simply being afraid to see where their hunger might lead them.

Often, people allow this to happen to avoid feeling disappointed. It strikes me as strange that we can live with other emotions, like sadness and fear, but most avoid disappointment at all costs. We really don't like to go there. Maybe it's the fact that disappointment is an emotion that rests squarely on the individual who is feeling it. You can't blame anyone else. It's internal. The connection to the Hunger square here is that those who squelch their hunger often do so to avoid disappointment.

The rationale seems to be that if we don't want much, we won't be disappointed. Whenever I say that in a speech, workshop, or seminar, I can hear people gasp in acknowledgment. The oxygen seems to leave the room for a moment. I once had a woman in an audience of a thousand people relate to this so intensely that she cried out, "You've just explained my whole life!"

In my surprise, I blurted out, "Is that a good thing?"

The woman realized that she hadn't allowed herself to want much from life, because she didn't want to be disappointed. That realization proved to be a cathartic moment for her. She vowed to rekindle her hunger for a better and more-fulfilling existence.

Think about reaching the end of your days on this earth. Do you want to reach that point wishing you'd reached higher? That's how my father felt, and he made me promise that I wouldn't follow the same path. You and I want to look back upon our lives and feel that we made the most of every talent, every opportunity, and every minute. That's why I share The Bigger Game with people and organizations around the world. If I can help one person think at life's end, *I went for it!* then I've fulfilled my own compelling purpose.

Psychologist Abraham Maslow defined the human hunger for meaning as the need for self-actualization. He developed "Maslow's hierarchy of needs," which defines prioritization of human needs. Commonly portrayed as a pyramid, this hierarchy depicts our most basic needs forming the broad base at the bottom, such as physiological needs, and higher-level needs, such as safety, love and belonging, esteem, and self-actualization moving up toward the top. That hierarchy has been described as "the path to happiness."

Self-actualization stands at the top of the pyramid. It's no surprise then that he believed, "What a man can be, he must be." (Obviously, this goes for women, too.) The hunger inside is what drives self-actualizing women and men to continuously strive for something more than simply what life hands them. They have a powerful desire to write their own stories rather than to follow a script written by fate.

When you feel a hunger to create a bigger game, whatever that game might be, you're seeking to self-actualize, write a meaningful life story, and serve your greatest purpose, whether its within your current situation or it requires a change to an entirely new environment.

If you've never stood on the Hunger square, maybe you need to turn up the dial, raise your expectations, and step right up. As you may have noticed in Ibrahim's bigger game, once he fed his hunger, he attracted allies and investments that helped him ship food, clothing, and medical supplies that greatly improved the lives of people living thousands of miles away.

STAY HUNGRY

Earlier I mentioned the legendary speech that Apple's co-founder and driving force Steve Jobs made at Stanford. In encouraging the graduating class to be self-motivated and unafraid of challenging the status quo or taking risks, he concluded that speech by challenging the graduating class to "Stay hungry. Stay foolish." As Jobs proved with his drive to create innovative products—and as Ibrahim Salih and Alice Coles also demonstrated in their own bigger games—hunger is a powerful force. It's a fire we want to keep burning throughout our lives, because it's what keeps us engaged and fulfilled.

To keep the fires burning takes courage and commitment, especially because it can be so darned cozy in our comfort zones. I've worked with corporate executives who, by nearly all other measures, have it made. They're at the top of their fields, set for life financially, respected, and in command. Yet they become avid players of The Bigger Game because they want fresh challenges. Some choose to play their bigger games within their organizations or outside their careers, in public service or volunteer groups. Others choose to leave their secure jobs and launch their own businesses or nonprofits.

There's one thing you can be sure of when you allow yourself to turn up the hunger dial: the status quo will no longer work for you. I've had people in my workshops tell me at the end that they either love me or hate me—for the same reason: "You've awakened the hunger in me, and now I have to do something about it!"

So, what are *you* going to create with the hunger inside of you?

● ✖ ●

COMPELLED BY A PURPOSE

The Compelling Purpose square is the place to go when you've identified your hunger, embraced it, and now want to find a way to
use it to create your bigger game. This will be something that lives
deep inside you. Think of this purpose as being like the music waiting
to emerge from inside a child blessed with a beautiful voice, or the
stories built up and ready to flow through the pen of a gifted writer.

Your compelling purpose is something so powerful that once you
identify it you can't *not* do it, any more than a great singer can quiet
her voice or a great writer can lock his stories inside. This irrepressible
desire or force within comes from a place of deep knowing. It's very
much a part of who you are or, perhaps more likely, who you want
to become. One of my workshop participants put it this way: "Your
hunger pushes you. Your compelling purpose pulls you." Brilliant!

This square is your first step toward fulfilling your destiny. You're
on the way to something beyond business or life as usual. So, the
time to step right up to this spot on The Bigger Game Board is when
you realize that you simply cannot ignore or put aside some powerful
desire, vision, or mission. To ignore it would be to deny who you are.

When I do workshops for global corporations, there are often skeptical and resistant participants. They've grown weary of change initiatives and flavor-of-the-week motivational programs. It doesn't take long to spot them in the crowd. Loud sighs and big eye rolls are usually the first indication. Loud snoring is another clue. (Okay, that hasn't happened!)

I can't blame them. I feel their pain. Then I do my darnedest to win them over. They don't always embrace The Bigger Game, but every now and then, someone crosses over and becomes a true believer and enthusiastic player. Usually this occurs when the person does a quick two-step dance on the board, first on the Hunger square and then the Compelling Purpose square. One of the great examples of this was a man who came into my corporate workshop with all of the enthusiasm and eagerness of a disruptive teen sent to the principal's office.

After the second day, however, he came up to me before the workshop, and I swear he was giving off sparks he was so fired up. At first I thought he'd overdosed on Red Bull or espresso shots. He admitted to me that he'd signed up for the workshop only because his boss thought he'd become disengaged from work. When he told me why, I was reminded about the importance of seeking first to understand before judging how he'd behaved the day before.

He'd been dealing for years with a teenage son who was addicted to drugs. Few things could be more distracting or more tormenting. Finally, they'd found a rehabilitation center that had helped save his son's life. This father was so moved by their work and compassion that he wanted to create a bigger game to help this rehab program reach out to even more young people. He'd undergone a cathartic moment in our discussions. As he told me about his newfound purpose, we both teared up. I was so happy for him. I was also so grateful that my workshop had helped trigger his activism and enthusiasm. It took a very bold action for him to reveal this personal information to me. The courage that it takes to feel deeply and share feelings with others is not business as usual for many of us. Hats off to this inspiring leader.

Your compelling purpose can play out within your career, your personal life, or the world around you. It can and probably will change over time and throughout your life.

THE THREE ATTENTIONS

Our hunger and compelling purpose usually focus on one of the three attentions. This concept was brought to me through The Coaches Training Institute, which informed much of my work. Thank you, CTI. The first is self, which I'm sure you're familiar with; if not, you should introduce yourself to . . . your self. This is the area we focus on instinctively from birth as a survival mechanism. We're compelled to feed our hunger and thirst and other basic needs. We learn to cry or smile or reach out to get what we need, whether that's by bawling at the top of our lungs for a feeding or, a little later, pestering our parents for the new Super Mario Bros. video game.

As we move out of infancy and into childhood and through adolescence, we generally become more aware of the needs of the second of the three attentions, which is others. Our focus goes beyond merely the self and its desires. We grow more attuned, hopefully, to the needs of those around us. Occasionally, our hungers and purposes match up so that we find fulfillment in serving the needs of others, as in the case of Alice Coles and her fellow Bayview residents.

And finally, I hope, your attention level expands to include the last of the three attentions, which is the field. This refers to the world around you. You eventually become aware that the world around you has needs as well. You'll find your bigger game when your compelling purpose drives you into taking action. Now, that doesn't mean your bigger game must be altruistic, like Ibrahim's project in Africa, but your compelling purpose usually feeds a greater hunger than just your own. If your hunger and compelling purpose don't serve a hunger somewhere beyond your own nose, you very likely won't be playing a bigger game.

Say, for example, I decide that my compelling purpose is to transform the world's streets and highways from paved concrete to natural grass. That's right, the green, itchy stuff we rolled in as kids. It's unlikely that anyone beyond a few lawn-loving fanatics like myself would buy into my "green" mission, unless I produced something like scientific evidence that showed my grass streets and highways would stop global warming and improve the air quality of the planet dramatically. In that scenario, I might well have a bigger game that would be sustainable and impactful.

If you are chugging along with your bigger game and one day realize that it isn't going so well or that you're playing without partners, you might have to consider that your compelling purpose isn't matched to a hunger out in "the field." On the other hand, you'll know your bigger game is working when people eventually are lining up to stand behind you—to help you, to support you, and to cheer you on. Or another possibility is that there's dormant hunger out in "the field" that simply needs to be awakened. Who knew we needed smartphones? And now we can't live without them—a dormant hunger "to be connected" made tangible with these high-tech gadgets.

The game is on when you identify and pursue your compelling purpose. It tends to gather momentum and size as you go, the snowball effect, and you may find yourself drawn into a much bigger realm, beyond anything you might have imagined.

ACTING ON YOUR PURPOSE

Most actors make a movie, play a role, and move on, but Gary Sinise has had no desire to leave behind Lt. Dan Taylor, the Vietnam veteran he portrayed in the Oscar-winning movie *Forrest Gump*. His Academy Award–nominated performance of the tormented, disabled vet struck a chord with critics, audiences, and the actor himself.

Sinise often tells interviewers that he knows many veterans, some of them family members, who suffered physical and emotional damage in battle, and that his portrayal of Lt. Dan Taylor mirrored their experiences.

More than 15 years after that movie's release, Sinise remains a tireless advocate for not only U.S. military veterans but also children caught in war zones around the world. His efforts are his way of using his celebrity status and resources to serve his country, he says.

When not filming segments of his television series *CSI: NY* or working in other roles, Sinise travels across the country and to military bases around the world with his Lt. Dan Band, performing more than 30 concerts a year. Most are benefits or USO shows for American military troops and their families. His band also regularly performs at fund-raisers for individual soldiers with service-related disabilities. In addition, Sinise is the national spokesperson for the American Veterans Disabled for Life Memorial.

In his first trips to perform in Iraq and other regions devastated by war, Sinise often observed American soldiers giving supplies to children. He was inspired by those outreaches and decided to join them. He enlisted the support of a friend, best-selling author Laura Hillenbrand (*Seabiscuit* and *Unbroken*), to form Operation International Children, a nonprofit that provides school supplies, blankets, shoes, sports equipment, backpacks, and other goods to children in war-torn areas.

While Gary Sinise has never played The Bigger Game as far as I know, he certainly lives according to its principles. He's another natural bigger game player, one who's driven by a compelling purpose to serve as a resource and supporter of others. His purpose is so compelling that it has taken him all over the world and consumes much of his time away from his acting career, with no expectation of financial compensation for his efforts.

IT'S PERSONAL

One of the defining aspects of a compelling purpose is that it's personal. Gary Sinise was compelled to move from actor to activist and advocate because the role of Lt. Dan took him inside the life of a disabled veteran. He was drawn farther into that world by the powerful response to his character from veterans across the country. Once he was welcomed into their world, he saw the great need in their field, and it became deeply personal. He saw veterans as real-world heroes, and he became their champion by using his celebrity status to serve them. It was something he couldn't *not* do.

To be in a bigger game, you have to be compelled from the inside out, not outside in. In that mode, you can do amazing things. It's like having superpowers. You have more energy and drive than you probably have ever felt before. We've all heard the stories of good Samaritans who've somehow managed to lift cars or fallen tree limbs off people by summoning strength they've never had before. Some say it's due to an adrenaline rush, and that may be part of it, but I believe it's also the incredibly powerful knowledge that this is something that simply must be done. There's no other option but to do what would normally be extraordinary, but now is required.

Your compelling purpose is like a force of nature. It cannot be denied. You'll likely experience more than one compelling purpose in your lifetime. One may lead to another, or you may have a couple going at the same time. My two brothers and I share the one I mentioned earlier: our father's encouragement to make life a great ride so that we never looked back and wished we'd done more or reached higher. We never sat down and agreed that our father's lesson would serve as a compelling purpose that we all lived by.

My brothers and I took different paths, but over the years, we could see that each of us was determined to chart his own destiny. None of us ended up working for large corporations as our father had done. I came the closest, but whenever I felt myself being drawn into that comfort zone, I was compelled to walk away and strike out on my own. These days I'm compelled to support employees and teams within large companies and to help them become more engaged and creative with their work—for that is the goal of The Bigger Game workshop.

Your compelling purpose can take many forms. In this case, mine was almost a subconscious message that has played out through my life: to take responsibility for my own happiness and to always pursue what most fulfills and energizes me.

Take fair warning: once you're in pursuit and engaged in your bigger game, you'll probably have moments when you wonder what the heck you're doing. I left what was likely a very secure and lucrative career with The Cheesecake Factory to strike out on my own. Later, I turned down very good offers in the corporate world. Call me crazy, but also call me compelled by forces that can't be denied. I'm driven to make my life a great ride, to never settle, and to always be playing at least one bigger game. Now, that's just me. Many people, including Melissa O'Mara and Mats Lederhausen, have found compelling purposes and bigger games within their corporations. They, too, have enjoyed great rides. In fact, their bigger games brought new meaning and purpose, as well as profits, to the companies they worked for. I've seen this happen time and time again, when employees become more fully engaged and driven.

Earlier I mentioned Ruth, who attended one of my workshops for a corporate client in Australia. She told me that she'd long felt compelled to become an advocate and activist for change in that country's health-care system. She'd had a really bad experience with her own child in a hospital there, bouncing from one specialist to the next, having to repeat tests because all of those involved in her treatment weren't communicating with each other. Her goal was to make it easier for patients to access a "one-stop shop" for medical care.

She already had a great job within the corporation—she loved the company and her role in it. Yet she couldn't shake the inner voice telling her that there was a need in her country's health-care system and that she had the responsibility to use her talents and brainpower to address that need.

"I don't know how to do that, and I don't want to abandon a career that I've worked so hard to create," she said.

I assured her that she didn't have to give up her career with the corporation. I'm with Leonardo da Vinci, who seems to have lived a pretty full life. He advised us, "Make your work to be in keeping with your purpose."

I reminded my friend that she was employed by a powerful company that provides innovation in every aspect of business, including the health-care industry, and that she could work from within her corporation to make things better.

The beauty of her story is that when she went to her boss and told him what she wanted to do, he helped her create and execute her bigger game within the corporation. He recognized that this woman was engaged and compelled, and that her energy and passion were great assets for the company. Why not make the most of that resource? Why not tap the power of her bigger game and embrace it? Now the boss was also responsible for the bottom line. He took that into account, too, noting that the health-care industry was huge and innovative programs were in great demand.

THE TRIPLE WIN

Dare I roll out the *w-w* term? Yes, I think it's time: most bigger games are win-win propositions by their very nature, and this is yet another example of that. When a compelling purpose meets a need in the universe, it's always one for the w-w column. But here's the best part: you don't have to keep score when you play The Bigger Game. The victory isn't in the win. It's in the playing.

Although great outcomes often result from bigger games, the real payoff is the rich relationships and depth of meaning that come from a fully engaged life. Through Bob Pranga, Dr. Christmas, I met another person who has become very important to me.

One of his celebrity clients is Leeza Gibbons, who has become his friend as well. He and Leeza invited me to lunch one day while I was in Los Angeles.

Leeza, who then had her own syndicated talk show, asked me to explain The Bigger Game to her. She grasped the concept immediately and exclaimed, "I have a bigger game!" Given her long career in television and support of many worthy causes, I wasn't surprised. Still, I was surprised to learn about this particular project, which truly is a great example of a bigger game driven by a compelling purpose. Leeza's hunger arose from a "No, not that!" situation involving her mother when she became an Alzheimer's patient.

Leeza found back then that most nursing homes just weren't set up to provide the high level of care needed by the growing number of Alzheimer's patients and their families. Before her mother's death, Leeza promised her that she would tell her story and do something to make a difference for other individuals suffering like her and for the families who care for them.

She had no training in the health-care field, but Leeza had something every bit as useful: a powerful purpose. She didn't want her mother and others like her to suffer while the industry caught up.

The broadcaster and talk-show host didn't worry about how to solve the problem; instead, she focused on creating a solution. She also focused on her strengths rather than her weaknesses. She put her celebrity power into action and created a nonprofit organization in 2002: The Leeza Gibbons Memory Foundation. The primary focus of the foundation is Leeza's Place care centers in California, Illinois, and Florida, which provide free support services, resources, and programs for family members of people suffering from memory disorders or any chronic or progressive illness.

After Leeza told me about her bigger game, which continues to expand its outreach, I agreed to serve as an ally. To help her, I led The Bigger Game workshop for an evening session as a fund-raiser to benefit her cause. That event led to my being asked to deliver The Bigger Game team session for the Alzheimer's Association, which has its own bigger game to eradicate this horrible disease. Coincidence? I think not—and by now, you agree. In working with Leeza, I've seen the power of a compelling purpose that grows from the inside out.

Leeza's love for her mother stirred something so personal and so powerful that this television personality became a force to reckon with in an entirely new field of endeavor. Whether your compelling purpose inspires you to create a bigger game within your current place of employment, in your personal life, or out in the big ol' world, I encourage you to wrap your arms and legs and heart around whatever excites and compels you. You will win (self), others around you will win (other), and the world at large (field) wins—a triple win.

● ✖ ●

COMFORT ZONES FOR BETTER AND FOR WORSE

First let me say that I have come here neither to praise comfort zones nor to bash them. For decades, comfort zones have been misunderstood, maligned, and defended, but mostly abused. I mean, it's not as if they were war zones—or *Twilight Zones*—or even no-parking zones. Unlike those zone-family cousins, there's nothing inherently dangerous, scary, or unlawful about comfort zones.

Comfort is widely considered to be a good thing, right? So why do comfort zones often have negative connotations? They can serve us well on this sometimes extreme, strange, and chaotic planet. You have an inalienable right, for example, to tell the salesperson at Macy's that skinny jeans and Spanx are not in your comfort zone. When the burly guy seated next to you on the airplane wants to share his love of outrageous Japanese cartoons, I don't think anyone would blame you for firmly declaring that he's violating your in-flight comfort zone.

Seriously, the good comfort zones need to band together and hire the same public-relations firms that rehabbed the images of LeBron James after he left Cleveland and Angelina Jolie after she left Billy Bob. Comfort zones get bad press, too, but they aren't all bad.

They're simply habits, behavior patterns, states of mind, attitudes, routines, and default positions that serve our purpose at given points in our lives because we feel they reduce stress and give us security. Comfort zones can serve us well, but we need to be wary of staying too long and trusting them too much. Simply said, comfort zones can serve us, until they don't.

All of this is my way of saying that the Comfort Zone square— the top-left square but not necessarily your first stop—on The Bigger Game Board can be a very useful place as you play your bigger game. You shouldn't fear to tread on this spot. No guilt and no problem—as long as you remain aware, at all times, that a comfort zone can become a danger zone, or at least a place of diminishing returns.

When we were kids, my brothers and I played hide-and-seek for hours and hours. I had one favorite hiding place that was very cozy, and for a long time, nobody could find me there. But then, the inevitable happened. My brother discovered my hiding place—with me in it.

Apparently I thought he had a poor memory, because I went back to that cozy hiding place a few weeks later, during another hide-and-seek game. My brother quickly figured out where I'd stashed myself and dragged me from that place.

"Why'd you go back there when you knew I'd find you?" he asked.

"Because it's my *favorite* hiding place," I said.

So it goes with comfort zones. We tend to stay in them too long, even well beyond when they've served their purpose. Most of us are always in some sort of comfort zone. Often, we only leave one because we're stepping into another that offers greater rewards.

Comfort zones need to be assessed constantly with a sort of cost-benefit analysis. If a comfort zone costs you more than it serves your bigger game, then you need to leave it behind. Many people stay in relationships that have gone sour because they are so comfortable and leaving them is scary. We tend to create and cling to comfort zones to avoid risk when we fear the unknown. But avoiding risk isn't really the best strategy if you want to create a great life. Taking well-considered risks can be a very good move, as most successful people will tell you. Being comfortable isn't really where you want to be. Creating chaos and feeling unsettled can lead to breakthroughs and greater opportunities. In fact, true risk takers consider being uncomfortable, in itself, to be a comfort zone.

Yet, most of us tend to seek comfort physically and emotionally. The problem is that we aren't always adept at evaluating whether being comfortable is where we really need to be. Sometimes—and more often than we may want to admit—discomfort, especially in the form of change, is what leads us from bad to good and from good to great.

SATISFACTION HAS NO TRACTION

Early in my work life, I was quite happy as a struggling actor and part-time waiter in New York City. I didn't have much, but I didn't need much. That comfort zone served me well, and I had a nice run in that lifestyle, but eventually I realized that this comfort zone was probably preventing me from finding something much more fulfilling over the long term.

During the recession that began in 2006, millions of people lost their jobs. I had many clients who felt demoralized as their companies repeatedly downsized, firing people in wave after wave over several years. Most of those who felt they would eventually be terminated developed their plan B options, but they were reluctant to leave the comfort zone of a job until they were forced out, even though the working environment was miserable due to the constant stress.

One client in particular had been developing a sideline business for years to supplement his income. His "day job" actually paid less than his sideline job, but he felt he needed the security of the day job and the health benefits that were part of his employment package. The layoffs in his industry were so massive that any sense of security disappeared early in the recession. Still, he stayed in the comfort zone of a corporate job until he was finally pushed out the door in another round of cuts.

He mourned the loss of that job and the benefits for a couple of hours and then committed himself fully to his well-crafted plan B. He tripled his income within the next year, during the recession. Even better, he reduced his stress levels by 300 percent, despite being self-employed, because, finally, he was in control of his own destiny.

Thomas Edison said, "We shall have no better conditions in the future if we are satisfied with all those which we have at present." Being aware and alert to the nature of your comfort zones is critical if you are to play a bigger game. If you settle into a life or career without weighing the benefits and the detriments, then you run the risk of going on cruise control—or out of control altogether.

SHORT-TERM COMFORT

There has to be a payoff for squatting upon or leaving your comfort zones. We tend to stick with them when the known is less scary than the unknown, or when we've become reliant on short-term benefits. Drug addicts are an extreme example of a group that clings to comfort zones purely for the short-term high. Most know in their hearts that they're destroying their minds and bodies, but the immediate and intense pleasure payoff overpowers all reason and self-control.

Entire corporations do much the same thing when they become addicted to short-term profits. IBM stuck with its big-frame computers while the public went mad for desktops and laptops. General Motors and its companions in the big three (Ford and Chrysler) kept manufacturing gas-guzzling SUVs even as the motoring public went shopping for smaller cars and hybrids.

Still, there are companies and individuals who've found very profitable comfort zones over the long term, making minor adjustments when needed. Tiffany's seems to be a good example of that. Southwest Airlines is another major player that appears to have landed on a very profitable long-term comfort zone. This wildly successful airline embraces creativity and fun as part of its culture. Founder Herb Kelleher established that approach to business, and so far the payoff has been substantial.

ZONE AWARENESS

So the purpose of the Comfort Zone square on The Bigger Game Board is to provide a space where you can first acknowledge that you're in a comfort zone and then determine whether it's right for you in that moment and into the future.

One of my own habitual behaviors, a.k.a. comfort zones, is to be a worrywart. It's always been that way for me. I don't know why it's comforting, but it must be because I can be a world-class fretter. I'll wake up in the middle of the night, because my head is abuzz with all these minor concerns that suddenly seem like major crises. I can fall captive to those worries for hours upon hours, losing sleep, making my heart race, and destroying my mood for the entire next day.

I know the comfort zone of being a worrier is not serving me well. It stresses me out, zaps my creativity, and sucks the joy out of my life. I've learned to be more aware of this negative comfort zone. Have I completely abandoned it yet? No, but I'm working on it. Just being aware of it makes a huge difference. I'm learning to give it up.

The Comfort Zone square gives you a space in which to go through the same analysis. It's less expensive than seeing a shrink, and there's no time limit. We all have comfort zones that may need to be abandoned at some point. One of the corporate teams I coach with The Bigger Game realized this after standing on this square.

Their comfort zone gone bad was built into a weekly telephone conference with their higher-ups at headquarters. These calls covered a lot of ground, from new projects and innovations to the financials. In flush times, the team had fallen into a comfort zone of talking about the financials up front, because the news was usually very good and invigorating. But times changed during the recession, when the financial reports were bleak. Yet because they'd been in the "financials first" comfort zone for so long, they'd continued to discuss them at the beginning of the meeting. They soon realized that dealing with the bad news up front drained all of the positive energy from the rest of the meeting.

Finally, one team member recognized what was going on with this comfort zone and made a suggestion: "Why don't we talk about the financials at the end of the meeting instead of up front?" From that point on, the entire dynamic of those weekly meetings changed. First they discussed the exciting and positive new and innovative developments, and then, as the meeting wound down, they went over the financials in a much more hopeful and optimistic mood because they were aware that good things were in the pipeline. They still talked about the numbers, but the paradigm of the discussion was transformed.

The hunger for money and the quest for wealth and financial security create some very tricky comfort zones. Those driven by that common desire are often disappointed when money in the bank doesn't guarantee gladness in the heart. The old saw "Money doesn't buy happiness" has been supported by research. One report found that between 1970 and 1999 the average American family received a 16 percent raise in income (adjusted for inflation), while the percentage of people who described themselves as "very happy" fell from 36 percent to 29 percent during that same period.

Many of my clients and workshop participants come to me for help breaking free of the "more money" comfort zone, because despite their financial security they find themselves depressed, lonely, and unfulfilled. There are wealthy people who are perfectly happy and fully engaged in life, but most of them will tell you that their happiness is due to the richness of their relationships and the rewards of their work, not the size of their bank accounts or stock funds.

PITY PARTIES

Among the more infamous and insanely bad behavioral comfort zones are those for victimhood and self-assigned helplessness. Many people play the victim or refuse to accept responsibility when the going gets tough. Those comfort zones can make us lazy, dependent, and weak in the knees. No one likes to admit that he or she is playing the victim or shirking responsibility, but we do it nonetheless. Few would deny that those comfort zones are disaster zones for anyone who has dreams of a better life or a bigger game.

Just as the unexamined life isn't worth living (according to that wise guy Socrates), the unexamined comfort zone may not be worth occupying. Playing a bigger game requires self-awareness and self-determination. We must be willing to take calculated risks if all signs point to Go.

The key questions to ask as you stand on this square include the following:

* ✖ What are the rewards for sitting tight?

* ✖ What's the cost of remaining in the comfort zone?

* ✖ If I leave here, what better opportunities or possibilities are out there?

* ✖ Is it possible that I could find an even better comfort zone out there?

* ✖ What would an even better comfort zone feel and look like?

* ✖ Does this comfort zone serve me and my bigger game?

The problem with many comfort zones is that they aren't all that comfortable for those who cling to them. They're just less scary than whatever else is out there. We can find ourselves reluctant to abandon them even when we yearn for something more—even when we know our talents, skills, and brain matter are not being fully deployed.

SQUARED OFF

Some comfort zones have definite payoffs. Others carry a hefty price. The "I am perfectly comfortable not driving above the speed limit" comfort zone is obviously one with a positive payoff. On the other hand, "I'm staying in this abusive relationship because I don't want to be alone" is a very dangerous comfort zone. There's inner work to do here with the support of a compassionate ally.

I'd also encourage you to abandon any comfort zone that allows you to play the victim; the misunderstood genius; or the unforgiving wronged, bitter, and angry person. Yes, those are very cozy places to hide, but what's the long-term payoff? How can you hope to have loving relationships or to make a positive difference in the world if you've built walls around your heart and holed up like a hermit from the rest of the world? The good news here is that once you know this, you can dip into the Allies square and ask for help. We all need support, especially when it comes to dealing with our dark sides. I'm a huge fan of looking deeper into the sources of some of these comfort zones that get in the way of playing a bigger game.

We dig into a comfort zone when the payoff is good, but too often we refuse to leave it even when the rewards diminish and the costs soar. It's like staying in your first home for sentimental reasons even though the taxes have tripled, the roof leaks, the walls are covered with black mold, and a family of possums lives in the attic.

This is known as the comfort zone of denial, and it can be deadly. That said, leaving a comfort zone is rarely easy. Often, it's downright scary or painful. This explains why people don't leave abusive spouses or partners—and why people spend their entire careers in jobs they dislike.

Few people embrace change unless there's some clear-cut, no-money-down, no-interest, satisfaction-guaranteed-or-your-money-back assurance that the change will bring sweet rewards—or that if you don't change, you'll die.

As I mentioned earlier, my co-creator of The Bigger Game, the late Laura Whitworth, was a heavy smoker. As a very smart, perceptive woman, she knew logically that cigarettes weren't good for her health. Unfortunately, logic wasn't enough to convince her to abandon her comfort zone of smoking. Her addiction to nicotine and other chemicals in cigarettes was more powerful than her fear of the health hazards. The addiction took hold of her, and her body trumped her brain.

She acknowledged this to me and to those who attended our workshops. She used it as an example so that others could see that maybe their own comfort zones weren't serving them well. I'm sure you've known people who stayed with bad habits or in jobs or relationships that weren't healthy despite knowing that they were destructive. Getting them to abandon those comfort zones is extremely challenging. Often, the addict will break off a relationship rather than break a self-destructive habit.

Laura smoked cigarettes for many years. It took a very compelling force to make her give them up. During a workshop to train prison inmates as coaches for fellow inmates, she mentioned her smoking habit as an example of a negative comfort zone. After that session, a burly, scary prisoner pulled her aside, looked into her eyes, and said, "This workshop has given me new life and helped me survive inside these walls. You must stop smoking, because I need you back here. If you don't stop smoking, please don't come back."

Despite his menacing manner, this was a good Samaritan in disguise. He drove Laura out of her dangerous comfort zone. She went home that day, threw out her cigarettes, and put an end to her smoking days. The prisoner had found the Eject button, one that Laura had never expected. Sometimes we need a push from another person: someone to give us a compelling purpose to leave a comfort zone that isn't serving our best long-term interests.

"Saving his life was more important to me than saving my own," she told me.

WHERE DO YOU STAND?

Benevolent comfort zones are like plush bedrooms in five-star hotels. You feel satisfied, safe, and secure in the knowledge that there are few better places where you could be. Negative comfort zones are like a tall tree in a gator-infested swamp. You climb up and hang on, because what lies around you is scarier than where you are.

Many people don't stop self-defeating and harmful behaviors, because the payoff to remain with the known is stronger than the payoff for leaping into the unknown. Are you satisfied, safe, and secure, or are you just plain scared? That's one of the questions to consider as you stand on the Comfort Zone square on The Bigger Game Board. This is something you have to decide for yourself, and playing The Bigger Game can help give you the clarity to do it. As your bigger game unfolds, you should be aware that new comfort zones will form.

In my own life, leading workshops is a comfort zone. It totally serves my bigger game and my personal goals at the moment. Yet, in a few years I may feel that leading workshops no longer serves my bigger game if it has changed.

●　✖　●

CHAPTER 7

TAKE A
BIG *GULP*

I've been an actor and speaker for most of my adult life, so you'd think stage fright would no longer be an issue. Wrong! My stomach was swarming with butterflies and my head was whirling with insecurities a few years ago as I stood backstage at a huge international event for a Fortune 100 client.

Sweaty palms?

Check!

Dry mouth?

Check!

Wobbly knees?

Check!

This was a classic *Gulp* moment, equal parts terrifying and thrilling. Such moments feature the scary exhilaration that arises when you're compelled to do something totally outside your comfort zone but essential to your success. These moments most often occur when you're taking your first steps into unfamiliar territory. Risk is always a factor. Failure is always a distinct possibility.

They're a universal human experience, often beginning with our first steps. One moment you're safe and snug in the grips of a parental unit, and the next you're being released to the malevolent forces of gravity—often with a gentle nudge while someone across the room cheers: "Come on, you can do it! Walk! Walk!"

Usually there's a video camera trained on you to capture the moment of sheer embarrassment and terror. It's your maiden flight. You look down at your feet, then across the room to the target zone, and then back down at your feet, which seem very comfortable right where they are, stationary and secure.

"Come on! You can do it! Come to me!"

You do a baby *Gulp*. Then you take your first bold action and step forward toward your life as a biped.

Next up in your *Gulp* history is your first solo ride on a bicycle or your first trip off the high dive. Other classics include the following:

✖ The first time you have to read an English composition in front of the entire class

✖ Your first dance

✖ Your first time at bat, on the free-throw line, or guarding the goal

✖ Your first kiss

✖ Taking the wheel for your driver's test

✖ Your first sexual tryst

✖ The marriage proposal

✖ The walk down the aisle toward wedded bliss

✖ Signing your first home mortgage or car loan

✖ Heading for the hospital because the baby is coming

✖ Asking for a raise or promotion

✖ Signing the retirement papers

Spectacular *Gulp* moments make history. Benjamin Franklin flying his kite in the thunderstorm is a *Gulp* for the history books. Charles

Lindbergh's solo flight across the Atlantic in 1927 and Apollo 11 astronaut Neil Armstrong's first step on the moon in 1969 would certainly qualify. Daredevil Felix Baumgartner's record-shattering 24-mile, supersonic skydive in 2012 is one of the most recent big gulpers.

The *Gulp* square is the place where "I must" and "I can't" bump into each other and result in "I'm scared and thrilled at the same time!" But here's the good news about *Gulp* moments: As long as you're having them, you're pretty much guaranteed to be alive, breathing, and engaged in a bigger game! If you're not having *Gulp* moments as you play your game, then it has become a business-as-usual game. The *Gulp* square is on the game board to measure your level of thrills, passion, and OMG-ness!

That's what I told myself as I had an anxiety attack backstage with more than 600 high achievers in the audience from Japan, China, Australia, Thailand, North America, and our host country Vietnam. My topic for the presentation was the same as the subject of this book: "The Power of Playing Your Bigger Game." I'd been developing and refining the concept of The Bigger Game for about eight years at that point, so I knew the material.

I also knew that a roomful of MBAs with years of high-level corporate experience and exposure to wave after wave of flavor-of-the-month motivational and change initiatives can make for a very tough and highly critical audience. Then there were the cultural differences to consider. I could sense their skeptical thoughts: *Who is this American guy to tell me how to play a bigger game? What could be bigger than the game we're playing every day at work?* This is a comfort zone of my own, by the way. It's the zone in which I make stuff up about what others are thinking.

There were other factors feeding my self-doubt. For nearly a year prior to this event, I'd been dealing with the loss of Laura Whitworth. I wasn't sure I could continue presenting and building on The Bigger Game without her. This speech was my first attempt to go solo with the concept.

Taking a moment to assess my feelings, I realized that I wasn't so much intimidated or frightened as excited to be continuing our mission once again. Encouraging others to play The Bigger Game had become important and deeply fulfilling for me. I felt that this was truly one of my purposes in life.

My excitement and gratitude overwhelmed me to the point where I wasn't sure I could talk, which presented a problem for a guy about to step onstage in front of hundreds of people. In that moment something happened that's very typical of The Bigger Game experience. Inspiration took over. I remembered that it was Valentine's Day, the perfect day for being in love, whether with another person or with your life in general.

When it came time for me to step out in front of my sophisticated audience, I broke the ice simply by wishing them all "Happy Valentine's Day," and then, corny as it may sound, I said, "Will you *all* be my Valentine?"

They laughed, and I heard yes in a half-dozen languages. It struck me that The Bigger Game had no borders. I was both thrilled and humbled to be a part of something that has changed, and will change, so many lives for the better. That presentation was a home run and truly a revelation for me. After that international audience of top corporate executives embraced The Bigger Game concept, I realized the rest of the world would be open to it as well. Now when stage fright and insecurities come over me, I can go back to that moment of victory over my fears. I use that memory to move beyond *Gulp* and into gratitude. I realize that I'm not so much scared as excited and joyful, because I'm playing my own bigger game. In my own *Gulp* moments, I also summon up the recollection of my father saying, "At the end of your life, you want to look back and say, 'That was a great ride.'" It reminds me of my compelling purpose, which gives me the strength to kick into bold action.

Moments of doubt and fear mixed with excitement and anticipation are part of every bigger game. In fact, if you don't have some, you probably aren't playing a big-enough game. Sweaty palms and a faster pulse come with risk-related behavior. You'll likely have all sorts of questions and self-doubts rattling around in your brain:

✖ *I don't know how to do this.*

✖ *What was I thinking?*

✱ *I'm in way over my head!*

✱ *How did I get myself into this?*

Instead of backing away because of those nagging inner voices, you might try welcoming them as true signs that you're moving out of a comfort zone and toward a bigger game. Embrace them and acknowledge them in the moment. Fear is simply an emotion, a natural fight-or-flight response to a perceived threat. It shouldn't paralyze you or leave you unable to act. Instead, it should propel you into action. Fear, after all, is not just a part of life; it's a sign of life. If you can experience fear, it means you're still drawing breath, and as long as you can breathe, you can play a bigger game.

Consider fear a validation instead of an impediment. Use the energy generated by the emotion to move forward. Wallowing in fear and dread is its own comfort zone, and to leave it, you may need to step into the Hunger square and remind yourself of your compelling purpose. Then, move on to Bold Action, and you'll be back in the game.

THRILL POWER

When you enter Disney World, Universal Studios, or any other amusement park, you pay good money for the *Gulp* experience on roller coasters and thrill rides. Why do we want to trigger that sensation? What's the payoff? The rush of endorphins, your body's home-brewed version of morphine (*endorphin* means "morphine from within"), is certainly a big part of the attraction. Endorphins are powerful but short-term painkillers, and they also create a rush of pleasurable sensations. Our blood endorphins increase during workouts, sex, and times of stress. Some studies have found that endorphins are released during acupuncture and massage, too. Women experience a rush of endorphins to help block the pain after delivering babies; otherwise most would never have more than one child—or so I'm told.

So when you feel a moment of head-spinning trepidation coming on, go with it. The endorphins released can reduce anxiety and depression while giving your self-esteem a boost and improving your overall mood. Good things usually come from *Gulp* moments. They come when we challenge ourselves to stretch and grow, to do more and to be more.

You and I came into this world with certain unique talents and gifts included, like a new car with the performance package or a new computer with the video-game player bundle. If we want to grow those gifts and talents, we have to move out of comfort zones and take bold action. In between lies the gulf of *Gulp*. It's an intimidating gap between where you are and where you want to be—no, where you *must* be—if you're to pursue your passion and compelling purpose.

GROWING PAINS

If you're not gulping, you're not growing. Like bad-tasting cough medicine, it's a trade-off, a little bitter taste now to make you stronger in the days ahead. Playing a bigger game is all about learning and growing. There are four well-defined stages of this process with the gaping gulf of *Gulp* between the first two and the last two. You may know this because this concept has become almost common knowledge these days, and yet it bears repeating because it so gives us hope as we move forward in our bigger games.

Four Stages of Learning

1. Unconscious Incompetence. This is the clueless stage in which we don't know what we don't know. (I've never been in this position, of course. Or maybe I was in it and just didn't know it? Just kidding!) This stage is a comfort zone for most, because ignorance is bliss. The problem is that what you don't know can hurt you. Sooner or later, most of us realize that we don't know nearly as much as we thought we did. This realization even strikes a high percentage of college graduates, especially when they finally get jobs in the real world. Suddenly, all that theory runs smack-dab into the reality of how things really work or don't work. When that happens, the wiser souls move into the next stage, sometimes organically and magically.

2. Conscious Incompetence. In this stage, the lights come on. We know what we don't know. Or at least we have some inkling that we don't know it all or nearly enough. If you haven't hit this stage yet, you must be a teenager. If you reach this stage, it's because you found a clue. Maybe it was the co-worker who gently explained that the computer-software programming techniques you mastered in high school have been obsolete since the dawn of Windows 3.0. This is not a comfort zone, and that's a good thing. Ignorance may be bliss, but feeling ignorant isn't so hot. You should want to bust out of this stage as quickly as possible, but therein lies the gulf of *Gulp*—the gap between who you are and who you want to be, between what you want and where you are. This is the no-fun zone, but deep thinkers realize that you have to come rest for a spell here before making the leap—lump in your throat, sweat on your palms—to the next stage.

3. Conscious Competence. This stage in the learning process lies across the gulf of *Gulp* from conscious incompetence. This is the stage where the dancer knows the routine but still has to watch his feet or the guitar player who knows the song but still keeps an eye on his fingers. Once you're at this stage, you've acquired the information you need; you just haven't programmed it fully into your subconscious search engine. You're the second-semester typing student who still reverts to being a hunt 'n' peck plodder now and then. You're the basketball player who still needs to walk through the plays or the new driver who bounces off the occasional curb. You need to put knowledge into practice, and once you have mastery, you move into the final stage at the top of the learning ladder.

4. Unconscious Competence. Welcome to cruise control—well, maybe it isn't *that* easy, but this is the flow stage, where you master the knowledge and the practice. You're fully engaged and in control. You don't look at the keyboard when you type. You can whip up a Manhattan without checking the cocktail guide. You know exactly how to rebuild a Fiat engine (I really did this once) without once referring to the manual. Victory is yours!—until you get promoted, move to a new department, and return to a state of Unconscious Incompetence!

ANATOMY OF A _GULP_

Your _Gulp_ response to moments that are equal parts thrill and chill is hardwired into your brain's most primitive, reptilian regions— a group of nuclei deep in the medial temporal lobes, near the base of your skull, known as the _amygdalae._ (It sounds like some sort of Tolkien beast, doesn't it? _Beware the Amygdalae!_) This is where the brain processes memory and emotional reactions. In other words, it's _Gulp_ central.

Because the amygdalae are home to both memory and emotional-response nuclei, they set off fear alarms when you get into situations that trigger memories of scary stuff. This brings up the ages-old survival response that dates back to caveman days, featuring the classic three _F_ options: fight, freeze, or flee. Fortunately, there are other portions of the brain that work more like certified public accountants than teenage drama queens. These kick into gear to analyze the situation without the shrieking alarms and anxiety. If your built-in alert-analysis system determines that your life isn't actually in danger, you still get the sweaty palms, dry mouth, and butterflies in your stomach, but you squelch the urge to throw punches, go into ninja stealth mode, or run for your life. Instead, you go into _Gulp_ mode.

Let's say you assessed your life, realized you were in a cushy but unfulfilling comfort zone, identified a hunger for something more, and figured out your compelling purpose. This sent you off on your quest for a bigger game, but you had no idea how to make it happen and you realized there were certain risks involved.

That would put you and your sweaty palms squarely on the _Gulp_ square.

Now you have a couple of options. If you give in to your fear— also known as "_false emotion appearing real_"—you'll likely do a quick meltdown and go running like a scared puppy back to your old comfort zone. Distinguishing between real and perceived danger is the key here. When you're playing your bigger game, the things that seem scary aren't actually life threatening. Most of the time, the worst that can happen is that you'll feel embarrassed and maybe lose some money. That's not fun, but it's also not a deathblow. How many billionaires have lost millions along the way? From what I have read over the years, many.

You always have another choice when facing a *Gulp* moment, which is to call to mind why you walked up to the ledge in the first place—your compelling purpose—and to use that passion to leap onto the Bold Action square like a bigger game big person.

PLAYING AT THE UPPER LIMITS

A friend of mine compares this to his first experiences as an indoor rock climber. Since he lives in the Midwest, he'd never done serious rock climbing until he went to Upper Limits, a renowned indoor rock-climbing gym in an old grain elevator in Bloomington, Illinois. He wore the required safety harness but still found it incredibly daunting to scale the 65-foot "rock wall" created inside the former grain silo.

Every move, either up or down, required leaving a (relative) comfort zone and moving across a gulf of *Gulp* to a new handhold and foothold. For each and every inch of progress, he had to fight off the alarm screaming from the amygdalae, "You're gonna fall and kill yourself!" My amateur-climber friend had to train himself to quiet that alarm and focus instead on the task at hand—and foot. Bold action was required if he wanted to achieve his goal of overcoming his fears, exercising his body, and climbing the wall safely.

His was a bigger game aimed at strengthening his body and his mind, and he discovered, while talking with its owners, that the climbing gym was an even bigger bigger game. You see, the Upper Limits climbing gym was created by a young couple, Chris and Pam Schmick, when both were still in their 20s. It was in the mid-1990s that Chris, a boilermaker and avid rock climber, and Pam, an avid Chris fan who overcame a fear of heights to become his "partner in climb," decided to create their own indoor rock gym on the Illinois prairie lands.

Theirs was a bigger game on a grand scale, but they had no idea how to make it happen. There were no blueprints for transforming massive old grain elevators into state-of-the-art climbing gyms. It was a brilliant idea. All they needed was a plan and the money to make it happen. They also had very little to invest other than their time, energy, and effort. With a loan from Chris's grandmother and another from a friendly bank, they made a down payment on the nearly 200,000-square-foot fixer-upper (emphasis on *upper*) that had been abandoned to pigeons and other creepy creatures for more than ten years.

You and I probably can't even imagine how many *Gulp* moments were involved in transforming the nearly indestructible white elephant packed with rotted soybeans and trash into a world-renowned climbing center that hosts international competitions and has been hailed by major media, including *Sports Illustrated* and both the Discovery and Travel channels. After more than three months of cleaning 12 tons of trash from the building, the Schmicks's compelling purpose left Chris hanging from a rope in the silo for another five months as he drilled an estimated 100,000 holes for handholds and footholds into the concrete walls.

The couple did most of the work themselves, with help from friends and a few hired hands, as well as a local architect who welcomed the challenges of this unique project. Nearly two decades later, the Schmicks are still avid climbers and bigger game players. Thanks to the success of their first Upper Limits, they've opened two more indoor-climbing gyms in Missouri.

Getting past the *Gulp* was essential for the Schmicks, just as it is for anyone who is compelled to play a bigger game. They learned to use the energy from their fear to move ahead with bold actions. As the Upper Limits founders discovered, when you're playing a true bigger game driven by a compelling purpose and passion, you're so wrapped up in it that many *Gulp* moments pass before you even realize they were there. They still occur, but you deal with them quickly and with relative ease because you're so fully engaged—mind, body, and spirit.

IN THE FLOW

The noted author and psychologist Mihaly Csikszentmihalyi describes this experience as the state of "flow." He calls it an "optimal experience"—and perhaps the ultimate feeling of happiness. Most of us have been in this wondrous state at some point in our lives. The luckiest, who are passionate about our work, experience it on a daily basis. Think back to your childhood, when you were caught up in some sort of play and completely lost track of where you were and the passage of time. Maybe it was just a game of Monopoly or Candy Land, a pickup baseball or basketball game with friends, or hide-and-seek with the neighbor kids. You may have found yourself in trouble with your parents because you were late for dinner or stayed out after dark. Still, it was probably worth the grief, because that feeling of flow is so exhilarating. Athletes call this "being in the zone." Writers, painters, sculptors, and other artists often experience the same feeling, in which they become so engrossed in their work that it's almost as if they're being guided by some sort of higher power. This is definitely a high level of unconscious competence, in which you stop thinking about what you're doing and simply let it flow.

Many avid bigger game players even come to see *Gulp* moments as welcome signs that they're about to enter a state of flow. They embrace the *Gulp* because they know that the next step for them is perhaps the Bold Action square, and then their game is on and they're living their dream. This is all about the journey, of course. Imagine how great it would feel to wake up each morning driven by a compelling purpose and passion for what lies ahead.

ADDICTED TO ACTION

Once you've made the leap over the gulf of *Gulp,* you'll likely become addicted to new experiences, which means bigger and still-bigger games. Fears will still surface, but you'll recognize them instantly as nothing more than emotional alerts to take bold action. At this point, challenges become stepping-stones. The gulf of *Gulp* becomes less intimidating with each bigger game.

Just look at those natural bigger game players, the Schmicks. Once they took on and mastered the challenge of converting the first abandoned grain elevator into an acclaimed indoor-climbing gym, they gained the confidence to create two more.

The more bigger games you play, the more skillful you become at moving past fear because of the faith and confidence you have in your abilities. You also learn to assess situations and your progress honestly and accurately. You accept mistakes as part of the learning process. Believe it or not, you'll probably learn to laugh at your biggest flubs, at least after a little time has passed.

I have one last reminder for helping you over the gulf of *Gulp.* Earlier in the book, I noted that life is a game and that it's all made up. There's power in believing that—so much power, in fact, that I named my company It's All Made Up, Inc.! I believe we can and should create the lives we want by continuously playing bigger games. *Gulp* moments occur when we let past experiences create doubts and stir fears, yet what is past is past. Don't look back. My advice instead is to live in the moment, because you really have no idea what the future will hold either. Instead of waiting for the future to come, why not make up your own life as you go?

We do this anyway. We create mental pictures for our lives. Sometimes these are good, sometimes they're bad, but they're always "all made up." These mental pictures are the basis of our created experiences. Remember, your life goes in the direction of the thoughts you carry in your mind and the words that fall out of your mouth.

So why not make up your life as you go? The Bigger Game is yours to play as a way of creating that life, one in which fear isn't an obstacle but, instead, a welcome sign that you're alive and well and fully engaged in writing your own story.

● ✖ ●

CHAPTER

8

THE BEST INVESTMENT YOU'LL EVER MAKE

Gina Paigen, a passionate player of The Bigger Game, calls herself "a seeker and a lifelong investor." An avid reader, hungry learner, and fearless free spirit since her teenage years, she's not one to linger for long in any comfort zone. She has continuously invested time and energy in her psychological, intellectual, and spiritual growth, as well as in her mental and physical well-being. In her first 50 years on this planet, Gina worked at various times as a theatrical-lighting designer, a professional percussionist, a member in an all-girl rock band, and a photographer. After a divorce, she has also raised two children on her own.

I believe Gina was a natural bigger game player even before she actually attended her first workshop with us. This is a woman who goes all out, investing everything she has in everything she does. Although you would be correct to think of Gina as a very artistic person, one of her most challenging bigger games was in the rough-and-tumble construction business. In 1995, she went into that trade with her then boyfriend, who had a background in window installation and construction.

"I was working on a degree to become an art teacher when I met a guy who was doing construction, and he asked me to help him out, so I did—for 17 years," she told me.

The closest Gina had come to this sort of work was designing and building theater sets earlier in her life. Still, she fearlessly jumped in and taught herself the fenestration business after they launched their company, Infinity Glass, in Buffalo, New York. Gina found that she enjoyed the challenge of learning something new every day, creating her own accounting system and managing the company's finances, bonding, and insurance. When she couldn't figure out how to do something, she called allies and friends in the industry for advice. The couple built their small business doing historic restoration, renovation, and new construction, specializing in custom wood, metal, and glass restoration.

About nine years into their business partnership, Gina and her boyfriend ended their relationship, which she said had turned contentious. Gina took over Infinity Glass, and when a big contract to renovate city schools came up, she launched an even bigger game. She created a sister company to manufacture custom and historic wood windows, doors, and glazing systems. Both businesses qualified for minority contracts because they were owned by a woman, and Gina took full advantage, pursuing work wherever there were opportunities.

While that seemed like a good idea at first, Gina struggled to run both businesses with limited finances and resources. Finally, in 2006, she realized she had to either shut down both companies or take a bold action. She was down to only eight employees, and combined revenues were less than $1 million. Infinity Glass had a large volume of work in the pipeline but lacked the resources and cash flow to perform adequately.

Her second business had been created to fulfill contracts for a major reconstruction program by area schools, but once that project was done, there wasn't much demand for their products and services. A major recession had kicked in. Work had slowed for their primary business, too, in part because they'd failed to market it adequately while they were busy with the new endeavor.

Rather than give up, Gina upped her game. To finance upcoming work, she borrowed from personal resources and came up with a creative idea to find the rest. She made allies of three larger contractors she'd worked with, offering each a discount for early payment. The immediate influx of cash provided the boost they needed, even though it cut into profits.

Once her companies were out of crisis mode, Gina made another assessment to see what further investments were needed to increase manpower and machinery. Infinity Glass spent about $50,000 for woodworking equipment, buying some at auction and leasing others. The business also upgraded its electrical system to handle the new machinery, which helped speed up production and improve quality.

As a result of those investments, the business grew to 50 employees, and revenues topped out at nearly $5 million. That's not the end to Gina's story, nor were her construction businesses Gina's final bigger games, but let's pause for a second here and look at the Investment square, where she and many other players made critical decisions about their commitments to whatever game they were playing.

TWO-LEVEL SQUARE

There are two levels and many dimensions to this spot on The Bigger Game Board. First of all, as your Bigger Game gets under way and progresses, it's likely you'll be investing money into it, especially if it's a business. Other potential investments may include your time, effort, commitment, and focused attention. Then the second area of focus for investment is you, the player. To become the person you want to be and to take your bigger game where you want it to go, you'll find it necessary to invest in yourself in many, many ways.

I tell myself that every day—especially when the topic of physical fitness comes up. I'm not a slacker, but I am not a big fan of going to the gym. My preference is to get my heart rate up by water skiing or doing some other strenuous activity that's also exciting and fun.

I need a very compelling purpose in order to invest in exercise at a gym, even if it's a home gym. The fact that my pants don't fit can be a compelling purpose, and a good one. So is the fact that my work demands that I travel around the world on airplanes and eat in restaurants, so I need to maintain a strong immune system. I also need to be fit enough to stand for hours leading workshops and giving keynote talks. I'm compelled, then, to go to the gym to keep playing my bigger game—which is the teaching of The Bigger Game.

When I lead workshops for teams and organizations, the Investment square feels like home because so much of what participants want to talk about is the investments they're willing to make to advance their bigger games. The number one and two investments they identify are time and money, of course. What's interesting is that time and money are major comfort zones, too. We can easily fall into the trap of not pursuing our dreams because we don't have the money or the time. But if we're truly compelled, we'll find the money and make the time, or make the money and find the time.

Just as Gina realized in her construction companies, most entrepreneurial bigger game players often lack cash flow and resources. But, as her story illustrates so well, bigger game players don't hang out long in the comfort zone of "Well, I just don't have what I need to continue." Instead, their creativity and innovative thinking kick into gear.

Gina went to her allies in the business and came up with ways to get the cash and resources she needed to take her stagnant businesses to a new level. She assessed her situation and took bold actions to make those investments. While time and money are the most common investments we tend to think of, there are many others. In business, we invest in relationships, for example, with our customers, suppliers, partners, and others who are essential to our bigger games.

There are also long-term investments that may not produce results right away but help sustain and grow the business over the years. These include advanced-training programs; continuing education; and involvement in local, state, and national professional organizations. Then there are those investments that come from deep within: your heart, soul, blood, sweat, and tears—and full commitment of all of your resources to your bigger game. These are the investments from within that will show up when one is compelled by a bigger game.

GOING ALL IN

Because this is a two-level location, the questions we ask on the Investment square are also twofold:

* *What do I need to invest in myself as the player for the sake of my bigger game?*

* *And what do I need to invest in my game?*

Every investment you consider and make is for the sake of either you or your game—and often it's for both. When you're deeply committed to your bigger game, you're so compelled that you'll invest even beyond what you might do simply for yourself. Earlier I told you that my co-founder, Laura Whitworth, finally gave up smoking because a participant in her workshop for prison inmates reached out to her. He got to Laura by telling her that she was needed by him and others who were impacted by her work. Laura might never have stopped smoking for herself, but she stopped cold turkey for her bigger game and its beneficiaries.

The successes of activist Alice Coles, in leading the fight against the prison and then revitalizing the impoverished Bayview community, also offer many examples of investments made. Her rural community only knew struggle and suffering for many years. They couldn't see a better way until some of them created a bigger game, after finally determining that they would no longer stand to be overlooked and neglected.

Alice and her allies had only high-school educations, yet they invested many hours in recruiting experts, talking to the media, and educating themselves in complex matters such as writing grant applications. As a result of those investments, they defeated the prison and, upping their game again, fought for the revitalization of their entire community and the lives of their residents. By the way, Alice and her team also had to invest in each of those residents before moving them into their new homes. They had to teach them how to maintain their apartments and residences so that the rebuilt community could be sustained. To help them pay their rent and mortgages, Coles brought in job-training programs and helped residents match their skills to businesses and trades. They invested heavily in raising the level of responsibility and consciousness of those in the community.

The long-term game to transform Bayview continues to this day, of course. Coles and her allies have been working for more than a decade to revitalize the community after hundreds of years of neglect. The economic recession set back their efforts, and the fight for federal dollars has only become more difficult because of cuts in federal programs and increased competition from other needy communities clamoring for government assistance.

"We are struggling big time," was Coles's early-2013 assessment of her bigger game in Bayview.

While nearly 200 Bayview residents from 74 families are living in new housing in the 300-year-old community, more than a dozen individuals are still living in the old shacks, some of which lack plumbing, electricity, or both. Sadly, a husband and wife recently lost their new home after defaulting on their mortgage, so they have moved back into one of the shacks, Coles said.

"The old shacks are right across the street from the new village, reminding us how far we've come and how far we have to go," explained Coles, who is still writing grant applications to spur economic development and alleviate the blight and impoverished conditions that are still part of Bayview.

Coles has invested decades in her bigger game, and she's not about to give up on her town or on her belief that we all have a responsibility to each other.

"I don't take no for an answer," she said. "I don't think there is just one door. I think life is made up of many avenues. If we can no longer get the big grants, we will work to get the smaller grants. Bayview must sell the success we've had to sustain future growth."

Alice Coles is all out. She has invested her life in serving her community. That's what impresses me so much about this inspiring woman: the long-term investment she has made. Patience is a lost virtue for so many individuals and leaders in government and business. If change doesn't occur within a few weeks or months, they give up and walk away. Wall Street is the home of short-term thinking, but it's a malady that's spread into all other areas of our lives.

INVESTING IN HUMAN CAPITAL

The comfort zone of short-term gain is a serious pitfall for many bigger game players. Fortunately, Alice Coles isn't one of them. Many of the organizations I work with blatantly say, "We don't have the resources and time to invest in our people. We just need them to do the work to generate bigger outcomes and sales." I cringe every time I hear this. When I feel bold and courageous, I counter their contentions by telling them, "You don't have the time to *not* invest in your people. They're the lifeblood of your organization. Please reconsider."

When I introduce The Bigger Game to organizations, they often seem to come to a greater understanding that investing in their people pays dividends over the long term. The same is true of investing in yourself while playing your games. Many times, players find that the biggest investment they must make, at least initially, is in preparing themselves by clearing their minds and perceptions, learning what they don't know and what they need to know, and identifying skill sets necessary for success.

You'll need to clean out the clutter of your past games; clear the deck; prep your family and friends for the game ahead; and, last but not least, make sure you are mentally, physically, emotionally, and spiritually prepared for what lies ahead. I encourage players to take a look around with fresh eyes prior to starting. I find it can be helpful to do an Investment square checklist before takeoff.

POWERFUL QUESTIONS

* *What from my past experiences do I need to clear out or clean up so I can play this bigger game?*

* *What do I need in order to begin?*

* *How do I need to grow?*

* *What skills do I need to master?*

* *What weaknesses do I need to shore up?*

* *What strengths can I build upon?*

* *Am I physically, mentally, emotionally, and spiritually fit enough for this game? What do I need to do to become fitter in each of these areas?*

* *What financial investments do I need to make at each stage of this game?*

* *Do I have enough time to invest in this game?*

Once your bigger game is under way, I'd advise visiting the Investment square at least every couple of months to ask questions such as these:

* *Where do I need to invest more of my time and focus?*

* *Now what skills do I need to sharpen or acquire to sustain this game?*

* *Do I need additional financing to move to the next level?*

* *What resources do I need in order to keep growing?*

* *Is this game still personally compelling?*

* *How much more do I want to invest before moving on to my next bigger game?*

STAYING INVESTED

Alice Coles will tell you that there's no such thing as playing The Bigger Game on cruise control. She and her allies have done incredible things for their community, without a doubt. Yet she's still putting in long hours, pouring all her energy into sustaining Bayview and its residents. Alice, who has given presentations with me in order to share her wisdom, has never stopped investing her time and effort in her community. In recent years, she has played her game on a larger stage, as a speaker who inspires others with her commitment and spirit.

Let's return to Gina Paigen, another bigger game player who knows the Investment square well. I want to continue with her story, because this courageous and irrepressible woman also serves as an example of someone who never stops investing in herself and her bigger games. When she assessed her construction businesses in 2012, Gina asked the final question on the previous page: "How much more do I want to invest before moving on to my next bigger game?"

Her company had taken on a project that proved to be "disastrous" financially, and she'd been unable to fully recover. Gina decided it was time to find a more compelling purpose for her life. She'd taken courses in entrepreneurship at the SUNY Buffalo Center for Entrepreneurial Leadership a few years after going into the construction business. She'd later become a mentor for younger entrepreneurs through the same center, and she'd discovered her new compelling purpose in that role.

"I realized I had more of a gift for mentoring than for entrepreneurship," she said.

Gina had been feeling a hunger "to find work that came from the soul." She'd been dealing with a family crisis, and she needed that sort of work to sustain her. Mentoring young entrepreneurs fed her hunger. She knew that she was making a contribution to their futures, sharing with them her experience and knowledge. When she assessed the payoffs she received from mentoring, Gina realized that she had a passion for bringing value into the lives of other people.

She invested in that new compelling purpose by enrolling in a class at my personal and professional coaching alma mater, The Coaches Training Institute. On her first day in her first class, Gina observed the two leaders and afterward concluded, "I want to be in the front of the room, doing what they do for their students and those they coach."

Soon, Gina was fully invested in her new bigger game: to bring value to her clients and the world around her. She became a certified coach and then went through more training in leadership and spirituality. Her coaching and leadership-development business is Infinity Impact, which focuses on developing conscious, creative, collaborative, and purpose-driven leaders. As she notes on the Infinity Impact website, "We believe that when we align organizational vision with an inner sense of purpose, we tap into a potential where the whole truly becomes greater than the sum of the parts."

While devoting her energies to her new business and building up her individual and corporate clientele, Gina also made serious investments in her own growth and development. For a long time, she had quietly dealt with the emotional and psychological trauma she'd suffered as a result of physical and sexual abuse. Gina had worked with professional therapists for years to manage the shame she carried from those experiences. In her new bigger game as a personal and professional coach, she decided to go public in hopes of inspiring and helping other women who'd suffered similar abuse.

Her incredibly brave investment in that regard was a presentation she made titled "From Fear to Forgiveness to Forward" at a TEDx Buffalo Women event in 2013. (TEDx is a very successful "thought leader" regional conference.) Gina had been involved in theater, but she'd always preferred to work backstage. The thought of speaking about her most personal experiences to a live audience was terrifying to her, but she felt compelled to do it—truly a *Gulp.*

To help her through the TEDx talk, Gina tapped into the expertise of friends and colleagues who generously worked with her on its content and coached her performance. "When I finally got onstage, it felt like a collective process because of all the help I'd received," she said. "There were all these people standing there with me."

Gina's TEDx talk, like her coaching work, reflects her compelling purpose, which is to foster true connections between people and organizations. "It's about evolving human consciousness; living full-on and loving full-out; breaking down walls between gender, race, nationalities, and religious preferences; and recognizing that we are part of this larger cosmic web that runs through the universe."

SHARING AND CARING

I've offered the stories of Gina Paigen and Alice Coles to you in this chapter, because they're great examples of bigger game players who are continually investing in themselves and their compelling purposes. They're also part of a bigger movement that's all about investing in the greater good, the "shared value" movement. When you make an investment, whether in yourself or in your bigger game, your goal is to create greater value for one or the other, or even both. Shared value in business occurs when companies develop socially responsible business strategies so that both their bottom lines and the greater good are served. It was first defined by Michael E. Porter of Harvard Business School's Institute for Strategy and Competitiveness.

He found that businesses can invest in improving their productivity while preserving natural resources such as water, air quality, and oil. Yet another form of shared value involves businesses supporting economic development, infrastructure like highways and drainage systems, and government services, because they also serve the greater good. Others have described the concept of shared value as "doing well by doing good."

One of our trainers for The Bigger Game workshops in Korea brought the shared-value movement to my attention. Hyunsook Kim said playing a bigger game creates shared value. It is also a self-hunger serving an outside, or "field," need. Corporations like Nestlé have been credited with investing in programs that serve as examples of shared value. They also qualify as bigger games in my book. The Swiss food-and-beverage company, with more than 280,000 employees worldwide, recently rolled out the Nescafé Plan, a $350 million program to provide more than 1,200 coffee farmers around the world with agricultural training, 50-million high-yield disease-resistant plantings, and a reliable market for their beans.

Nestlé's plan doubles the amount of coffee it buys directly from farmers and their associations over the next five years, eventually purchasing 180,000 tons of coffee from around 170,000 farmers each year. The program brings value to Nestlé in the form of a steady supply of high-quality coffee beans while increasing the income of rural farmers and their communities, as well as easing the stress on their lands by teaching them more environmentally sound agricultural practices.

Another major corporation, Walmart, has undertaken its own shared-value bigger game by working with its thousands of suppliers around the world to reduce product packaging, which will not only save billions of dollars but also reduce the carbon footprint. When companies like Pepsi, Nestlé, and Walmart invest in bigger games that are shared-value plans, they produce triple wins because they positively impact the companies, their customers, and the world we live in.

My own experiences with shared value in bigger games includes The Coaches Training Institute, which, as I noted earlier, was co-founded by Henry Kimsey-House, Karen Kimsey-House, and Laura Whitworth. These three wise and compelled people were eager to train others so they could become effective coaches themselves. Initially their goal was to have a few workshops each month in the San Francisco area, but their investment of knowledge, research, time, and effort resulted in something of such great value that demand far exceeded their expectations. They'd had no idea that there would be so much hunger for that type of training. CTI is now in 25 countries. More than 35,000 people have gone through its training program, producing benefits for CTI, its graduates, and those out in the world whom they coach and serve.

As I noted at the beginning of this chapter, there are so many dimensions to the Investment square, and shared value is one of the greatest rewards. Your investments can range from the hours you spend developing your bigger game and carrying it out to the financial resources you put into it—or the additional training and education you go through in creating and sustaining it. You'll likely continue investing in your bigger game for as long as it plays out.

Keep in mind, too, that this is also the place on the game board to ask, "Is my heart and soul deeply connected to my bigger game?" There's no correct answer, but you should always be aware of it so that you can make adjustments to ensure that you're always aligned with your compelling purpose. I encourage you to also remember to always keep investing in yourself. This includes your health; your knowledge; your finances; and your emotional, physical, mental, and spiritual strength. The world needs bigger games, and for them to exist, we need dynamic, healthy, and passionate bigger game players.

● ✖ ●

ALLIES ADD UP TO A BIGGER GAME

Mary McDonough played in her first Bigger Game workshop about nine years ago. She is a professional and personal coach who has supported our trainings and other events from time to time. It's always good to have her, because Mary doesn't just know our material, she lives it—and in a big way.

If her name seems familiar, it's because you may have seen it roll by on television or movie-screen credits over the last 40 years or so. Mary is an actress who first became well known for her role as little red-haired Erin Walton in the beloved television series *The Waltons*. She has appeared in many other television shows and movies over the years. Mary has worked also as a director, producer, and author of her memoir *Lessons from the Mountain: What I Learned from Erin Walton*.

These days, Mary is writing her second book, working as a personal and career coach, and spending many hours as an activist and supporter of causes related to the physical and emotional health of women and girls. She's also very active in organizations that promote research and understanding of lupus, the chronic autoimmune disorder with wide-ranging, varied, and debilitating symptoms.

Mary has had this cruel and painful disorder since the early 1980s but wasn't diagnosed until 1991. Despite the challenges of lupus, Mary has remained active over all these years with her many bigger games. I've always been impressed with her great spirit, her empathy for others, and her ability to sustain herself and all of her bigger games.

Naturally, I'd thought about featuring her in the Sustainability square chapter of this book, but as we talked about that, she shared something that made her much more of a fit for this chapter on the Allies square. Mary said she often finds herself with a foot on each of those squares, because "having allies is one of the biggest ways to sustain yourself."

AN UNLIKELY ALLY

You might naturally think that everyone and everything that serves as one of your allies comes from a positive and benevolent position, but that's not necessarily the case, as Mary's story illustrates.

"Lupus, the disease, is an ally for me," she said. "It's huge."

Mary was diagnosed with lupus in 1991, after suffering for nearly ten years. Lupus has a variety of symptoms, including hair loss, sores in the nose and mouth, chronic fatigue, rashes, headaches, chronic pain, arthritis, and joint and muscle pain. Someone with lupus might have one or two of the symptoms, or all of them. It varies widely from person to person. Mary is in remission now, thankfully, but she suffered for years. At first, she considered it a curse, but she came to see it as an ally in her bigger games.

"It wasn't until I embraced that I had the disease that I actually got better," she said. "I never wanted to say I had lupus at first because I felt it gave the disease too much power. Somehow I thought it would keep the disease closer and I would continue to have it, but that thought process created denial. Once I acknowledged I had lupus, then I could work on finding ways to cure it and manage it."

Lupus became an ally, because it forced her to take stock of her life, Mary explained. "It forced me to slow down and brought me into my own self-care. It put *me* in the equation."

Mary said, like many people, she had often fallen into the comfort zone of not wanting to put herself and her health needs ahead of her family, nonprofit work, or her career. This is the comfort zone of selflessness many women fall into. Lupus forced her to face the fact that she had to take care of herself first so that she could continue her nonprofit work, her career, and the role of wife and mother.

"A lot of times we feel we have to be selfless and put everything we have into our work or our families, but when I became sick, I had to bring the focus back to myself. I realized that if I didn't have any energy, I wouldn't be able to help anyone or play my bigger game. Adding myself to the equation gave me a way to find healing and self-care, which is essential for what I want to do in my life," said Mary.

This is like the airline moment when the flight attendants instruct adult passengers to put on their own oxygen masks before assisting children on board. This is against the protective nature of most adults. Yet, it's true that if the adults can't breathe, they won't be of much use to the children.

Another of Mary's challenges is finding balance among all of her bigger games and her relationships. She works with many nonprofit groups while also coaching, acting, writing, and multitasking as a wife and mother. Like many of the women she works with in all of those roles, Mary relies on allies to help her balance out all of her responsibilities and interests. Many of these allies serve on the staffs and boards of the charities she works with. In her personal life, her allies include her husband and members of her longtime circle of friends who meet for coffee, share their lives, and serve as each other's sounding boards once a month.

"They are absolutely my allies," she told me. "I call them often. We create plans for the entire year, and we check in on each other to see how it's going. We are very supportive of each other."

THE DREAM TEAM

We all need allies who help us stay in our games and on top of them, too. The Bigger Game is not solitaire. You wouldn't play Monopoly or Twister by yourself, would you? It's a group effort. By definition, it's not truly a bigger game if it's something you can do alone. You must have allies to play, in the same way that you must have air to breathe. Thus, The Bigger Game Board features an Allies square, a place to hang with the buds, the posse, and other likely suspects.

Your bigger game can be as big as life itself, and to go that big, you'll need more than a little help from your friends—and probably your foes, too. You'll want to enlist the assistance of those whose talents and resources complement and enhance yours. You also would be wise to see those who might stand in your way or slow you down as sources of motivation and inspiration.

Feel free to be Lincoln-esque and acknowledge that your bigger game will be "by the people" and "for the people." The more friends, family, and fans who play alongside you, the more you'll enjoy your bigger game and the more impact you'll have with it. In my experience and from what I've observed of many other bigger games, most benefit from the snowball effect. As you roll out your game and it gains momentum, it expands exponentially as you pick up more and more allies who are drawn by your passion and purpose.

The Allies square is where you go to create friendships and be inspired by people. Once there, you identify those whom you hope to have standing with you, behind you, on top of you, in your way, and up and down the road. Then your mission is to invite them to join your game by sharing your passion and purpose, and helping them to discover their compelling purposes through playing alongside you.

Your dream team can include anyone who can help you by cheering you on, offering expertise, encouragement, resources, and guidance. Your allies might include your teachers, coaches, mentors, financial backers, co-workers, bosses, therapists, doctors, dentists, lawyers, accountants, and mechanics. Those who are served by your bigger game are allies, too. So count your customers, clients, audience, target market, readers, listeners, and fans. The obvious allies for most people are their parents, siblings, and other loved ones. You may find it helpful to create a list of the people in your life and, next to each name, write what sort of ally you hope that person is or will become. To help you identify your allies of all stripes, I've put together a list of various types of allies and their roles. Feel free to add your own as you compile your dream team.

Here's my allies starter kit:

Family and Friends

You're cherry-picking in this category. This is easy pickings, because these allies are already there for you. They're on speed dial and your smartphone's family-and-friends plan. They know you and, for whatever wild and crazy reason, may even love you. (Stranger things have happened, right?) If something matters to you, it will likely matter to them. That's a blessing, one that you should embrace wholeheartedly while pursuing your bigger game.

I encourage you to involve your family-and-friends allies in every aspect of every bigger game, from start to finish, through the ups and downs and ins and outs. These near-and-dear allies can be counted on to give you good feedback, because they aren't afraid of losing your friendship—or at least they shouldn't be—if they have to tell you something you don't want to hear.

That's one of two important points I want to make about this category, and it applies to others as well. The first point is that you should allow your allies to be honest and up front with you. The second is that you should be prepared to serve as their ally, too. Always remember that if you expect to make "withdrawals" on your ally accounts, you should have already made "deposits" of support and understanding. Family and friends may love you unconditionally, but they need nurturing, too. And, again, you should welcome their honest feedback without holding grudges or resenting them, because they truly care about you and want the best for you.

A few years ago, I hit a very tough stretch. I lost my uncle, my mother, and my 15-year-old dog, and I also became very sick—all within a few months. The stress, coupled with an infection, triggered a physical and emotional meltdown. I landed in the hospital for a couple of days.

Then, a few weeks after recovering, I had a major panic attack. My first call went to my business-and-life partner, Chuck Lioi. I unloaded a couple of truckloads of my angst on him. Whining and self-pity may have been expressed in detectible quantities. To his credit,

Chuck was compassionate and attentive to my needs for a good 20 minutes. Then he let fly with the best "Get your act together or let's stop this business" tirade I've ever received. Chuck went ballistic, but in a benevolent and healing way.

Basically he told me that if I wanted to do good and meaningful work, he was there for me always—but only if I took proper care of myself; asked for help when I needed it; and took full responsibility for getting my act together physically, emotionally, and mentally.

I thanked him and put in calls to my doctor, chiropractor, and therapist, maybe not in that order. Chuck was the perfect ally in that situation and many others. He was a true partner, one who cared enough to say, "Enough is enough!" He gave me empathy and support, but he also provided a reality check.

Chuck stepped up and reminded me of my compelling purpose, and then told me that I'd never be able to fulfill it if I didn't take care of my mental and physical health. Thanks, Chuck! I needed that wake-up call!

My other huge allies, earlier in life, included the pastor of our church and the other leaders and members of our youth group who were involved in my first unofficial bigger game, our mission to Appalachia. And, of course, in the creation of The Bigger Game, my greatest ally was Laura Whitworth, followed by her CTI co-founders and all of the folks within that great organization who guided, encouraged, and prepared me for my coaching career.

Even though she passed away many years ago, Laura still serves as my ally today. My memories of her and the driving passion to "awaken people to their greatness" always help to remind me of why I continue to do what I do. You should feel free to list as allies any departed family and friends who still inspire and motivate you. I'm a big believer in drawing strength from those who have come and gone but left their mark on our lives and the world around us.

Thinking of Laura also motivates me to keep building upon this bigger game by expanding the influence and reach of our co-creation. Whenever I feel discouraged or a little lost or my energy sags, I watch a video she once made. In it, Laura expresses her compelling purpose with such intensity and love that it always fires me up. It's not an exaggeration to say she is one of my strongest allies, someone who sustains me in The Bigger Game bigger game.

Prospects, Clients, Customers, and Constituents

As a bigger game player, you normally have someone with a need that you intend to serve, whether it will be the diners at your restaurant, the customers of your corporation, the beneficiaries of your nonprofit, or those who enjoy and benefit from your artistic endeavors. To put it in cold, hard economic terms, they constitute your target market.

You may also consider them important allies, because your bigger game exists to serve their needs while feeding your hunger and fulfilling your compelling purpose. When Mary McDonough attended one of The Bigger Game workshops, for example, she came as a client whom I considered an ally. Today she is very much an active ally on my dream team.

It's very much a win-win situation, because we've both benefited as individuals and as a team. Before we met, Mary was already a very busy, heavily involved, and seriously engaged lady with a strong social conscience. She was a natural bigger game player. Attending the workshop simply gave her some very accessible tools for her work as an actress, director, producer, activist, and advocate. "I'd done different sorts of training programs and workshops before The Bigger Game, and I'd done a lot of soul searching and assessment," she told me. "The game board is a great way to check in and look at where I am in my own bigger games. I can assess which squares I'm on and where I want to go next. It's just an easy concept to put to use."

Many of those whom I first meet as workshop clients or audience members for one of my keynote speeches go on to become serious allies. But even as clients and audience members, they're allies because in working to serve their needs I get to do what I love. They make me want to be better, which helps me increase the value of what I offer.

Co-players

Co-players are allies who've signed on to your bigger game. Many are actual partners in your bigger game if it's a business, nonprofit, or organization of some sort. Again, Chuck qualifies as my co-player, because he's my partner in The Bigger Game and in life. We're both in it 100 percent, meaning we both work full-time to nurture and grow the same bigger game, which is The Bigger Game brand. While he's the only ally so fully invested, we do have other co-players. Adora English and Jess Ponce of Media 2x3 are media consultants and branding experts who help us with marketing and public relations. They're in the game 100 hundred percent with us, even though they have other clients, because they're committed to our compelling purpose.

It's a very good idea to recruit co-players for your bigger games, because if your energy level drops or you fall into a comfort zone of being too busy or overwhelmed, your co-player can challenge and motivate you. Left to my own devices, I can fall victim to a less-than-hungry level of motivation, and I've been known to lose the charger for my compelling purpose.

Another perfectly good reason to recruit at least one co-player is that we're relational beings. We're hardwired to form cooperative alliances to accomplish more together than we would alone. And finally, it's just more fun to have someone else along for the entire ride, right . . .

. . . Chuck?

. . . Adora?

. . . Jess?

Champions

When I think of those who champion my bigger games and those of other players, I always picture in my mind a group of hyperexcited football or soccer fans sitting in the front row of the stands, wearing jerseys and painted faces and screaming their unabashed support and encouragement.

Yes, they're a lot like soccer moms; stage moms; and those crazy dads who scream at any referee, umpire, or official who dares to call a foul, pull a card, or throw a flag at their little darlings. There are bound to be allies on your dream team who fit into several categories. It's likely that most of those on your friends and family list will qualify as champions as well.

Grandparents are great champions when we're young, because they don't feel they have to discipline us or regulate us in any way. They just get to build us up and cheer us on, spoiling us in the process.

Your champions are allies who believe in your bigger game all the way. They may even think you can do no wrong, so with the most avid champions you have to seek some balance by also listening to more pragmatic and slightly judgmental allies. But they're great to go to when you need a boost in morale and a double shot of confidence.

Champions in my life certainly include my family members and my closest friends. These folks may not be involved in your game, yet they're so committed to your success and supportive of your game that they qualify as allies and champions. I can say with gratitude that I could reach out to every member of my family at any given moment, and each of them would encourage me and offer support.

One of the biggest outcomes my mom and dad wanted for their three boys was to get along and support each other. My mom even mentioned this in a note she left for us to find after she'd passed away. It ended with these beautiful words: ". . . and be kind to each other, stick together, and support each other."

My parents succeeded in raising my brothers and me to be champions for each other. I'll always be grateful. We are truly living out their wishes. Both my brothers and their wives and children couldn't love me more. They're so supportive of the work I do and so *there* for me when the going gets tough.

I'm blessed to have a loving and supportive family. I don't take them for granted at all. I actively solicit their support, and I do everything I can to be worthy of their love and encouragement. You shouldn't be afraid to ask the same of your friends and family. People don't always know what you need or want. Some may feel that they'd be intruding to offer help. If you want champions, you can't be afraid to recruit them. Some may not feel up to the task, so you can train them and give them what they need to help you.

I have a few champions who have agreed to be "on call" for me. I can go to them on a moment's notice, when I feel they can help calm me or enlighten me or point me in the right direction. They love serving as my allies in this way. I encourage you to recruit your own on-call champions—people who are eager to support you when you need them.

You may be in the comfort zone of "I don't want to bother anyone" or "People are busy with their own lives." Again, I encourage you to ask; you'll be pleasantly surprised at how most people will be flattered and excited to serve as your champions.

Coaches and Mentors

The distinctive feature for this type of ally is expertise. Coaches and mentors know what you need to know in order to help your bigger game be all it can be. If you're lucky, they walk into your life. If you're truly hungry and compelled, you seek them out. Sometimes you find them in totally unexpected places, and more often than you might expect they may not even know that you've adopted them as role models from afar. Occasionally, you may not fully appreciate them or recognize their importance to your bigger game until you've been in it for a while.

As a Master Certified Coach (MCC) with the International Coach Federation, I could go on for pages about the power of having a personal coach on your allies team—not because you need one to be successful, but because a professional life or career coach can have a dramatic impact on your rate of development. If you're playing a bigger game, which you clearly are interested in doing, then having a professional coach will only enhance the game.

I believe in the power of coaching. Our lives follow our words and the thoughts that are in our heads. So if you talk to a coach weekly, which I highly recommend, then you're talking out loud about the life you want to create and the game you're eager to make real. So it just makes sense that your life will go in that direction. It just works.

Ask Cheryl Richardson, a fellow MCC coach and Hay House author. She has a weekly Hay House Radio show on Mondays called *Coach on Call.* It's a great source of support. Folks can call in and receive immediate coaching that's laser focused, because she's a truly gifted coach and wonderful ally. Cheryl is a master coach on self-care. In her book *The Art of Extreme Self-Care,* she offers brilliant insights and deep understanding of the importance and value of self-nurturing.

Mentors are wonderful allies, too. These are people who have done whatever it is you want to do. They offer advice and knowledge to help you avoid mistakes they may have made, which means that you may move along more quickly and with fewer challenges in your own game. I do lots of coaching and mentoring with bigger game players (a.k.a. leaders), both from the corporate and private sectors. I live to do this, of course, but I caution them that I'm not a consultant with all the right answers. I simply offer my perspective and opinions. They can decide whether or not to follow my lead. You have the same choice with your mentor allies. They're guides, but you can decide to follow your own path, too.

Even today, I have two key coaches whom I reach out to frequently. They help me keep my own blind spots and comfort zones in check, and they coach and mentor me in my bigger game: The Bigger Game. It wouldn't be happening without these folks in my life. I say, thank you!

Expert Resources

The late pioneer of "gonzo journalism," famed writer Hunter S. Thompson had an interesting motto: "When the going gets weird, the weird turn pro." I've taken the weirdness out of the equation and amended that to, "When your bigger game gets going, turn to the pros."

Not quite as snappy, but more effective!

Until the guys from Google figure out a way to implant their search engine into our brains—which will happen one day, I'm sure—you'll need to tap into the expertise of allies who possess specialized skills and knowledge in order to launch, build, and sustain your bigger game. Expert resources may include a tax accountant; a lawyer to help with contracts, estate planning, and lawsuits; a computer geek; a website designer; public-relations pros; and a parade of other people who bring expertise to your bigger game.

I noted earlier that Adora English and Jess Ponce of Media 2x3 are among my allies. They qualify for the expert-resource category. There are many media consultants and public-relations and marketing firms out there, but Adora and Jess are bigger game players and executive coaches. They share my compelling purpose of inspiring individuals to become fully engaged, socially responsible, and fulfilled by playing bigger games throughout their lifetimes.

Adora and Jess get me. They understand the energy and essence of The Bigger Game. So does my literary agent, Shannon Marven, of Dupree Miller and Associates, another expert resource who has guided me throughout the process of writing this book. The key to having a great team of expert resources is to find people whose purpose and passions are aligned with your own. You want them to have your best interests at heart. Your experts should be invested in the same outcomes and in your bigger game. My publisher, Hay House, is perfect for this book, because they're playing their own bigger game. They're dedicated to bringing positive and inspiring messages of hope to the world. Now that's something I align with. It's an honor and a blessing to be one of their authors.

Spirit and Nature

Have you ever strolled in the woods or walked on the beach and experienced a deep sense of serenity, peace, and oneness with your surroundings? There's now science to support this common sensation. Several studies have found that being in places of natural beauty actually boosts our immune systems. Part of the boost is from stress reduction. Just being away from your desk or work and in a quieter and more serene setting reduces stress. If you choose to go into the woods to do that, I'd recommend avoiding alligators, bears, snakes, and other "natural" stress inducers. One of our workshop participants realized this when he went for a walk in the Adirondack Mountains of upstate New York during a break. It was a soothing experience until a bear appeared along the trail and was coming toward him. Luckily, he and the bear went their separate ways.

Clawed predators aside, nature is generally an ally, even in ways you may never have realized. Scientists have found that chemicals released by plants to ward off insects also offer benefits to humans. (Don't ask me how that works; biology was never my best subject.) The Japanese have a term for the practice of enhancing their well-being by communing with nature. They call it *Shinrin-yoku,* or "forest bathing." Studies of this practice have found that forests and other natural settings with abundant plant life resulted in lowered heart rates and lower blood pressure, among other benefits. I co-led an amazing group of Japanese leaders in a yearlong leadership program. Our venue offered views of Mount Fuji. If you ever get a chance to see Mount Fuji, run, don't walk. This natural wonder is something to behold, revere, and cherish. Every morning we would step outside our rooms and bask in the majesty and power of her imposing presence. This grand vision stirred something in me that I didn't know existed. Every time I gazed upon the mountain, some new thought or insight would strike me. I keep photographs of Mount Fuji on my iPhone to keep those feelings of awe and wonder alive, and to remind me to slow down and honor the presence of Mother Nature.

Prayer and meditation; yoga; soothing music; and other sources of mental, physical, and emotional relaxation are also allies in this category. I also include my late father among these allies. I still talk to him when challenges arise. You may be thinking, *Rick talks to dead people!* That's not really the case. It just gives me comfort when I share my life with my father's spirit. He doesn't talk back to me (well, sometimes I do hear his voice). Still, when I'm trying to work out a problem, talking to him seems to move me closer to a solution. Maybe you've had similar support from your own "unseen friends."

My final suggestions for allies to be found in this category are dogs, cats, and other furry pets. (Maybe your goldfish, parakeet, or pet python works for you; if so, I'm not going to argue. I just take more comfort in furry, four-legged creatures.) In my own experience, just walking my dog Abby was always a treat, because it was a time when I slowed down and just enjoyed the moment. I also found it relaxing to just rub her belly while we sat on the couch together.

Again, there's a growing body of scientific research to support the notion that pets are good for our health. Some research has found that the levels of cortisol, a hormone related to stress, are lowered when we interact with our pets. There are also reports that serotonin, the chemical associated with a sense of well-being, is increased and both blood pressure and cholesterol are lowered in pet owners versus non-owners. There are many amazing bigger games that train dogs to be therapy pets to assist the elderly or those with post-traumatic stress disorder.

I once did a leadership workshop that used horse-training exercises as a metaphor for leading humans. (Talk about *neigh*sayers!) I quickly learned that you either bond with the horse, or you don't. In the end, my horse trained me! When my horse for the workshop finally began responding, I felt this powerful bond and waves of satisfaction, because this huge beast and I seemed to be in sync. I've heard other people talk about swimming with the dolphins in a similar way. I believe all living creatures are connected, and I consider them allies—maybe with the exception of snakes and rats, but that's just me.

Volunteers

If your bigger game involves nonprofit work or even running a political campaign, volunteer allies will be an essential component, obviously. Yet you may also be able to recruit volunteer supporters if you're running a business or some other for-profit bigger game if you make it clear that you'll reciprocate and help them when they need it. You can't be shy about asking for help. You may be surprised at how many people are willing to step up, especially if you eloquently express your compelling purpose.

When you demonstrate that you're excited and enthused about your bigger game, volunteers are drawn to you. Social interaction and group effort are hardwired into us. I've volunteered for many different organizations, and there's nothing quite like the communal feeling of working together for a good cause greater than ourselves. These are instincts that have helped us survive and thrive as a species. The key thought with volunteer allies is that you have to make it clear that you'll be there for the other person when the time comes.

Come In and Remind Me

This is usually someone whose support for you is unconditional, someone who's as driven to see you succeed at your bigger game as you are, and maybe even more. This is the person, or persons, who senses your needs maybe before you do, the Good Samaritan who finds you on the roadside or comes knocking just to check on you even if you haven't been in touch for days or weeks. Bigger game players can be susceptible to all of the pitfalls of frustration and despair that others experience, so you will need these allies. But you have to recruit them and earn their support, because there has to be an almost spiritual connection between you. These allies just seem to know when you need them to reach out to you.

Laura Whitworth and I served each other in this capacity. If we hadn't talked in a couple of days, she'd come calling. And I'd do the same. We just sensed when the other person was in need.

Now the second level of this category is the ally from within. I think of mine as a nurturing father; you're free to choose whatever image works for you. I summon his image and his voice when I need encouragement and motivation, and sometimes a kick in the pants. He reminds me to be authentic. He reminds me of my strengths in times of doubt. And he's always there to bolster my spirits, reminding me to stay in the game.

I generally check in with him at least once a week. His voice says, "This is such important work you're doing, and you love it. Let me tell you all the reasons why you should continue and all the ways you do love your game." When you're playing a Bigger Game, you'll hit days that are so daunting and challenges so overwhelming that you may want to run and hide under your bed. This is the strong voice that stops you in your tracks.

This source of inner encouragement is just as likely to say, "You need to take a break," as it is to say, "Keep playing." It may tell you to give your bigger game a rest for a while, focus on building your strength or your savings, and then assess your situation and hunger in a few weeks.

I've had clients tell me that this inner ally is like the coach who calls the bull pen and tells the relief pitcher, "We need you to win this game for us." Inner encouragement is critical, because sometimes you'll be the only ally available. There's great wisdom in remembering to be as good a friend to yourself as you are to those closest to you.

Naysayers, Competitors, and Roadblockers

I led a Bigger Game workshop many years ago for a senior management team that included some hard-boiled veterans of the corporate world. Just a few hours into our first session, one of them blurted out, "This bigger game stuff is incredibly simplistic. I don't see how it can be of any use to anyone."

Well, thanks for your positive feedback!

I let this naysayer get to me initially. I stewed about his critique that night. I was hurt. Insecurities roiled up. Yet when I woke up the next morning, there was a fire in my belly. I wasn't angry. Instead, I was very clear about why The Bigger Game is an important tool, especially for those who've become cynical and resistant to fresh approaches within the corporate culture. I realized that Mr. Naysayer and I were there to serve and grow each other.

I rocked the second day of that workshop. I have mostly rocked it every day after that, too. I came up with concepts, contexts, and content that had never occurred to me in the past. Mr. Naysayer proved to be a terrific ally, a gift that just kept on giving, because he inspired me to up my own game.

Just as Mary McDonough bravely declared lupus to be her ally, you may benefit from embracing your competitors, antagonizers, and archrivals. They can drive you to make your game bigger and better. You may not like them. You may even curse the fact that they're in your life. But anyone or anything that motivates you, fuels your passion, and stokes your fire is an ally in some way.

I'll remember Mr. Naysayer to my grave. I realized that he was evaluating The Bigger Game as a two-dimensional model rather than a three-dimensional experience. I had him stand up, and I walked him around The Bigger Game Board, which is on the floor during these workshops. Within a few minutes, he was having deep insights for himself and his development. There were comfort zones that didn't serve him well. He discovered a deep hunger to be more innovative in his work, and we identified a bold action he could take by having a conversation with his boss.

As I worked through The Bigger Game Board with this naysayer, other participants became more engaged. Working with him proved to be a triple win for me, him, and all of the participants. His resistance was such a gift, and the power of it was amazing. It's a source of dynamic influence when tapped. Consider that electricity exists in the atmosphere as energy unleashed. Without the resistance of a wire, which is simply a tool to slow down electrical currents and point it in a particular direction, we wouldn't have been able to harness the potentially deadly power of electricity and use it for good.

The brilliant Henry Kimsey-House first taught me the leadership principle that says resistance is our friend. You may have seen this applied in a comedy club. Professional comedians are adept at taking hecklers and making them part of the act, tapping the resistance and turning it into a more engaging and "alive" performance.

When you're playing your bigger game, tap into resistance and use it to energize you, firing up creativity and confidence. Don't get mad. Get creative. In fact, it could be that your own naysayer might have a point. You should consider that, too. Maybe there's something to learn from the resistor that will make your bigger game irresistible.

That's what happened with Mr. Naysayer in my workshop. By the end of it, he saw that the simplicity of the game provided a portal for entrance into more complex and enlightening personal awareness. He even came up with some great insights for making The Bigger Game more effective as a team-building model and a leadership tool. I became grateful for his willingness to express his criticism, but also to offer his thoughtful advice and guidance.

Allies can also include competitors, arch foes, and the clueless person whose own bigger game is parked in your space. Where would Hertz be without Avis? Coke without Pepsi? Leno without Letterman? Overcoming the challenges presented by competitors will make your success all the sweeter!

My former boss David Overton, founder of The Cheesecake Factory, embraced the concept of competitors as allies. He welcomed it when other restaurants moved into the same areas as his own, because he believed the more people who saw his restaurants, the more who'd want to visit them. He also felt that because there was usually a wait every night for seating at The Cheesecake Factory, the competitors provided an option for diners who couldn't wait to be seated. David clearly operates from an abundance perspective. He believes that there's plenty of success out there for all to share and rejects the idea that it's merely survival of the fittest or that there's only so much success available in the universe. This approach has been very successful for The Cheesecake Factory.

I shared the concept of naysayers as allies while leading a workshop on The Bigger Game for a group of church parishioners in 2012. One of the things I noted was that the horrible recession was actually an ally for many people. This statement drew some odd looks and denials from the crowd, of course. I made the point, however, that the recession forced many people out of their comfort zones. I noted that historically some of our nation's greatest companies, including Walt Disney Company, Hewlett-Packard, and Microsoft were launched during economic hard times, because people were forced to become more innovative and entrepreneurial.

I had noted in the workshop that several major companies and corporations declared that they wouldn't participate in the recession— meaning that they would continue to be innovative and serve their customers' needs while remaining positive about the future. Very simply, they weren't going to use the recession as an excuse to simply accept lower profits. Now even those companies were affected by the economic downturn, but many of them remained profitable.

At the end of the workshop, one of the parishioners thanked me for making that point. He said the concept of hard times applied to his own company, which had taken bold action during the recession. Profits increased during the global economic slowdown. "We, too, didn't participate in the recession," he said. "We continued to train our people. We had off-site motivational meetings, and we remained focused on the good work we offer our clients."

The recession became a huge ally for his organization. It forced them to become more efficient and innovative. They took responsibility for their own financial health and refused to blame the poor economy. Blaming is a very enticing comfort zone when you're negatively affected by circumstances beyond your control. The key to avoiding this is to look for new opportunities that arise so that events like recessions and tragedies can become allies in some way. Ask, "What can I learn from this event? What insights does this situation offer me?"

ALLIES IN ABUNDANCE

What would your life be like if you considered everything that happens to you, good or bad, and every person you meet, friend or foe, to be a potential ally for you and your bigger game? Think about the past and how situations that seemed horrible at the time eventually proved to have positive effects? Consider also the people who hurt you or tried to hold you back. Didn't at least some of those naysayers and foes make you stronger in the end?

If nothing else, it's always interesting to view life in this way: all the good stuff, the hard stuff, the sad stuff, and the challenging stuff that comes your way may serve your compelling purpose and help you to create your bigger games. There have been things in my life that I so wish hadn't happened, including my brother's battle with cancer. Yet I've come to understand how his ordeal brought our family even closer together, made us stronger, and uncovered our gifts to levels that we might never have reached without this shared experience.

Seeing cancer as an ally is a total stretch, and if you'd prefer to reject that notion, I understand. But what would life be like if you looked for opportunity in every challenge and for alliances in every relationship, good or bad. I'd suggest trying this approach for the next 21 days. Psychologists say it takes this long to create a new habit. You may discover that this approach changes your attitude and your life.

Finally, in searching for allies wherever you can find them, don't neglect the most important of all: the one who looks back at you in the mirror. I mentioned earlier that it's critical to be as good an ally and supporter for yourself as you would be for your best friends and loved ones. The next time you're on The Bigger Game Board, put one foot on the Assess square and another on the Allies square, and ask yourself, "What's my relationship with myself right now? Do I believe I'm worthy of a bigger game? Do I love myself? Am I as forgiving of myself as I am of others?"

I recently attended a speech by Louise Hay, founder of Hay House, and she shared this great insight: "You are going to be in relationship with yourself your whole life; you might as well have it be a good relationship." So look within for your greatest ally. It may require some work. We're often hardest on ourselves, and we tend to forgive others first. We see our faults and weaknesses in a harsher light than others see them. Most of us are more accepting of the flaws of our friends than of our own.

Almost every client I've ever worked with has some inner voice that says some version of this: "I'm not doing enough with my life." It's certainly challenging to play your bigger game with that thought going through your mind. But you should pay attention to it and use it as an ally to drive your compelling purpose and your bigger game.

I've gone there many times over the years, looking within at what might be holding me back. I've gained insights into my comfort zones and my insecurities and how they've impacted my life and affected my bigger games. This is looking at the dark side, because it's the shadowy area where optimism fades and fears and insecurities lurk. I don't enjoy thinking about this part of my psyche, but when I go in there and am honest and real with my feelings, it's like cleaning house; it makes a huge difference in my enthusiasm and effectiveness. It frees up energy.

Emotions are energy in motion. Unexpressed emotions are the source of disease and depression. The brilliant and powerful work of Lucid Living founder Leza Danly, who advocates a metaphysical and spiritual approach to life, has helped me understand the power of going deep into whatever emotion I'm experiencing, understanding the power of fully expressing it, and then feeling the energy flow on the other side. This is why some of us go to movies and have a good cry   simply to unleash our emotions and feel more alive in the process.

I love the name of her work, Lucid Living. How many people long to live a fully engaged, lucid life? I can't tell you what an amazing ally Leza has been in my personal growth and the growth of The Bigger Game.

❈ ❈ ❈

Have you ever noticed how we repeat patterns in our lives? We often keep creating the same experience no matter what we do to change the external circumstances. For example, I've moved more than 15 times. When I look at the reasons why I've moved so often, I realize that I was changing my locations when I should have been changing my thinking instead. I had it in my head that this place or that place would be the best for my career or my personal life, only to move and discover that I still had the same issues no matter where I went.

Therapists call this "doing a geography": moving so as to hopefully change one's life for the better. I've learned that the common denominator in all of my challenges isn't the place. It's the person: me. I've worked on accepting myself first, forgiving myself, and loving myself. In doing that, I've saved thousands on moving costs, and I'm much happier, too!

During one of my workshops, we were discussing the Allies square, and a participant quipped, "It's 'all-lies' to think that we can get through life without allies." We all laughed, and I thought it was a brilliant concept. So remember to look for allies in every situation and to turn even your enemies into sources of positive energy, while always being the best friend you've ever had.

● ✖ ●

SUSTAINING YOUR GAME AND YOURSELF

The widely admired CEO of PepsiCo, Indra Nooyi, is my choice to serve as the poster "person" for the Sustainability square on The Bigger Game Board. Her company's earnings per share have risen 36 percent since 2006, when Nooyi became the first female—and first vegetarian—leader of the nation's second-largest food and soft-drink maker. Since then the company's overall sales have nearly doubled to more than $66 billion.

But what I find most impressive is that these gains occurred while Nooyi was fighting a difficult battle to change PepsiCo's image and product line in order to ensure that the global corporation remains strong for many decades to come by serving the changing needs and interests of consumers who've become more conscious about avoiding sugar, trans fats, and salt in their diets.

Back when we first created The Bigger Game Board, *sustainability* was the term we used in reference to approaching your bigger game and your life from the long view. Our goal was to encourage players to go to this square and think about two things:

✖ *What do I need in order to ensure the long-term health and viability of my bigger game so that even if I were out of the picture, the game could thrive without me.* (Think Disney without Walt or Apple without Jobs. Their games are currently quite successful even without them!)

✖ *What do I need to do in order to sustain myself as a bigger game player.* (Think about remaining on top of your game by tending to your physical, mental, emotional, and spiritual health.)

I'm aware, however, that the term *sustainability* has taken on a new and more profound meaning related to our responsibility as citizens of the planet to maintain a triple bottom line: a balance among social, environmental, and economic growth. The term has become a buzzword applied to a wide variety of "green" objectives, some sincere, others not so much.

There's no little controversy over how to define *sustainability* these days. Economists, business leaders, real-estate developers, restaurants, farmers, automakers, scientists, and environmentalists all have their own take on it.

For purposes of The Bigger Game, I have a somewhat narrower definition that can incorporate the wider meaning if that's part of your compelling purpose. The Sustainability square encourages players to accept responsibility for the long term in both their personal lives and their bigger games. This position, then, is about maintaining and building upon your game once it's up and running, which also includes self-maintenance so that you'll be around for the long term, too.

Indra Nooyi's efforts to dramatically change the culture and product line at PepsiCo reflect her long-term approach to management and her belief in social responsibility as well. All of the major soft-drink and snack-food companies are under increasing pressure to make their products healthier because of concerns about rampant obesity and diabetes around the world. Sugary soft drinks, in particular, have come under fire from consumer health and nutrition advocates, and even politicians have joined in. New York City Mayor Michael Bloomberg banned sodas and sugary drinks over 16 ounces in his city, and other communities are likely to follow. A bold action for sure!

Whether you agree with Bloomberg's actions or not, few could argue that his actions have helped inspire a much-needed conversation about obesity and eating habits in this country. Because of health concerns and an aging baby boomer population, consumption of sodas has dropped steadily in recent years and sales have declined despite higher prices. While Coke, Dr. Pepper, and other leading soft-drink companies have all tried to counter this trend by developing sugar-free and lower-calorie sodas, as well as more sports drinks and fruit juices, PepsiCo's CEO has become a leading proponent of much greater change in the soft-drink and snack-food industry.

Nooyi, whose PepsiCo product line includes not just Pepsi and Mountain Dew but also Lay's potato chips, Doritos, Cheetos, and hundreds of other snack foods and drinks, has called for reduced levels of salt, fat, and sugar in those products and for the creation of healthier alternatives that still taste good. Nooyi backed up that bold action by hiring an expert on diabetes and nutrition research at the Mayo Clinic to lead research and development at PepsiCo. Her often-stated goal is to see to it that consumers never have to compromise taste for health. She has also advocated changing consumers' eating habits by making healthier foods tastier, more affordable, and easier to buy.

TAKING THE LONG VIEW

Industry analysts say that this is a profound shift, and Wall Street, which is mostly focused on short-term profits, has questioned her strategy. Some major stockholders have threatened rebellion, even calling for her resignation. But this bold leader has stood her ground, saying it's the right thing to do for the customers and for the future of the company, because the global consumer market demands healthier choices.

This is definitely a bigger game Nooyi is playing, a fact reflected in her mantra that PepsiCo is focusing on "performance with purpose."

Time and again, she tells her critics and supporters alike that she doesn't manage the giant global corporation for just one quarter; she manages it for the long-term future.

The Sustainability square on The Bigger Game Board encourages long views like Nooyi's. I can't imagine the pressure she is under from powerful stockholders who are interested mostly in short-term profits. Some have demanded that she split PepsiCo into two separate companies, one for soft drinks and one for snack foods, because they don't want to wait for her plans to unfold. Yet few would argue that this CEO is correct in looking ahead and deciding that her corporation must change its entire product line, soft drinks and snacks, in light of a changing world.

I'm sure Nooyi has thought about what happened to American tobacco companies when concerns about the health hazards of cigarette smoking resulted in a massive drop in the market for their products. She doesn't want to be known as the leader who allowed one of the world's largest companies to ignore changing consumer desires and tastes.

As she has noted in interviews many times, true leaders must take the long view, and so must those who play The Bigger Game. The most avid and irrepressible entrepreneurs, performers, and leaders in business, government, politics, religion, and every other arena are those who endure year after year, decade after decade. They're always at the forefront, because they always look ahead.

THE HITS KEEP ON COMING

The best natural bigger game players are easy to spot, because they're not one-hit wonders who burn brightly and then fizzle out. They endure, and so do their bigger games. Many of them are cultural icons, maniacal entrepreneurs, and legendary world changers. Others are quiet heroes known and appreciated in smaller circles. Their games often seem outlandish and brash, and even doomed at first, but they endure and, often, keep amazing us over decades and beyond.

In business, Ted Turner; Bill Gates; Steve Jobs; Oprah Winfrey; Sir Richard Branson; and the Google guys, Larry Page and Sergey Brin, are among the most renowned "naturals" when it comes to playing bigger games. They've endured, and so have their enterprises. In the political arena, Hillary and Bill Clinton, George H. W. Bush, Jimmy Carter, and Nelson Mandela are among those leaders and public figures who have continued to play important roles over the years because they've sustained themselves and their passion and purpose.

Examples of the next generation of natural-born bigger game players includes Facebook co-founder Mark Zuckerberg, Spanx creator Sara Blakely, and Instagram cofounder Kevin Systrom. It will be interesting to watch them and see if they master the Sustainability square in the years to come. Their games may change. They may drop one to begin another, and sometimes they'll even fail, but the naturals stay on the board and in the game.

Ted Turner took over his father's modest billboard business in Atlanta and used the cash from it to purchase radio and television stations and the Atlanta Hawks and Atlanta Braves, before creating the global cable news brand CNN. His other enterprises have included cable network TNT, the Cartoon Network, World Championship Wrestling, Ted's Montana Grill restaurants, and the philanthropic United Nations Foundation, among others.

Steve Jobs brought the world Macintosh computers and all things Apple and Mac, not to mention transforming Pixar into an animation powerhouse.

Sir Richard Branson's ventures have included Virgin Records, Virgin Megastores, Virgin Atlantic Airways, Virgin Mobile, Virgin Fuels, and the space-traveling Virgin Galactic.

Oprah dominated the television ratings for decades, created a hit magazine, and then went on to found her own cable television network, where she nurtures and develops other performers, shows, and movies. Now that network had some trouble finding its groove at first, but Oprah didn't bail it out. Instead, she took over the role of CEO at the Oprah Winfrey Network (OWN).

Oprah took the long view and is patiently guiding it through the rough years, leading the way with high-profile and highly rated interviews, most notably that with Lance Armstrong, which attracted an amazing 28 million global viewers—a high percentage of whom likely have never seen a bicycle race. Now most industry analysts believe OWN is coming into its own, especially with Oprah clearly demonstrating that she's in this for the long haul by increasing her time on the air and taking direct responsibility for its success.

By the way, one of the most critical challenges Lance Armstrong faced after appearing on Oprah's show and admitting to doping was how to sustain his nonprofit foundation, which is widely respected. Originally known as the Lance Armstrong Foundation, the cancer-research organization has raised more than $400 million since he formed it in 1997. I'm sure that Armstrong, a cancer survivor, considered his foundation to be a major part of his legacy, and it may be the only aspect of it that will endure.

I'm not making any judgments about Lance Armstrong. His tragic story does illustrate the challenges of sustaining a bigger game after its creator has moved on. Armstrong's global fame as an athlete and the compelling story of his survival and victory over cancer have served as the focus of the foundation's fund-raising and marketing. Long before his confession, the charity's damage-control team had to contend with the in-depth report of its founder's drug use by the U.S. Anti-Doping Agency.

Imagine the challenge the charity faced, and will continue to face, in separating itself from its founder and continuing its good work while still honoring Armstrong's role in its creation, the selfless efforts he has made, and the millions of dollars he has personally contributed as its largest donor. The foundation's first major step to sustain itself was to have Armstrong resign as chairman of the board. The new board then changed the name to Livestrong Foundation, further distancing itself. This was followed by the removal of any mention of Armstrong's cycling career from the foundation's website.

Armstrong's organization has done wonderful things, and it should continue its good work despite the damage done to his reputation. Whether or not that happens, we can all learn important lessons about sustaining our own bigger games from this story. One of these lessons is that maintaining your reputation is critical to sustaining your bigger game. It's indeed heartbreaking to witness Lance's fall from grace.

CHANGE IS GONNA COME

There are many places on The Bigger Game Board where you can begin playing. Sustainability is the square you go to when you want to think about making sure your game survives and thrives over many years—and you with it. If the *Gulp* square is where you go to conquer fear, this is where you go to conquer, or at least fend off, the ravages of time and the changes that come with it.

Markets change. The economy rises and falls. Consumer tastes fluctuate. Public opinion shifts. New technologies arise. Calamities and disasters create need where it may not have existed before. You change, too, whether because of age, health problems, a different perspective, or a new and more compelling purpose. The Sustainability square is your place for pondering what you can do to stay in the game, whatever your game may be. There's no right answer, only the answer that the square awakens in you. You may even decide that it's time to change the game completely.

This is where you come up with strategies for victory, playing like a grand master in chess who looks beyond the next move to the next and the next and the next. This is about maintaining and building upon what you've accomplished so far. The questions you ask here run long and deep, both personally and professionally:

* *What do I need to do to ensure that what I've built will endure beyond my time on this earth?*

* *What skills do I need to build so I can keep playing my bigger game?*

* *How do I build my physical, mental, and emotional strength so that I'm around to enjoy the fruits of my labor and to keep my bigger game nurtured and growing?*

SUSTAINING THE PLAYER AS WELL AS THE GAME

As I noted earlier, this is a two-part square, much like the investment square. The first part deals with sustaining the impact of your bigger games so that they endure and serve as a legacy. The other is about taking care of yourself mentally, physically, emotionally, and spiritually. Living authentically and in balance is a crucial aspect of playing The Bigger Game. Players must avoid burnout and social isolation if they hope to play joyfully throughout their lifetimes. As the player, you serve as the engine that drives your bigger games, so to keep that engine running you must look after all aspects of your mind, body, and spirit.

In a sense, this square is both the janitor's closet and the workout gym on The Bigger Game Board. You stop here to consider how well you're maintaining your game and your life. The goal is to sustain yourself and your enterprises so you can continue to pursue your compelling purpose. Sometimes this is easier said than done. Many players, whether they're entrepreneurs, social activists, government leaders, or corporate-change leaders and innovators, have to support themselves and their bigger games with bill-paying labor. Challenges are often part of the process. Those who sustain themselves through the hard times often emerge stronger, wiser, and more confident for the long term.

How many successful app creators labored in corporate IT departments before striking it rich? Aspiring fiction writers often pay the rent as advertising copywriters or college English teachers. Novice filmmakers may have to make commercials or wedding videos. Celebrated director Quentin Tarantino had humbler beginnings. He has often said that many of his award-winning movies were inspired by films he watched while working his shift at a video store. As a natural-born bigger game player, Tarantino has built a long and sustained career in Hollywood across three decades, and he's still going strong.

Most of us have to pay dues and deal with challenges that we can learn from before we hit our strides and find sustained success.

That's part of the game, too. You may even look back upon your days of struggle as a blessing because of the lessons learned along the way. A key to surviving and thriving as a player is to always be mindful of where you are on the game board and why you're in the game in the first place. After years of denial and lies, Lance Armstrong finally admitted that he had lost his way. Winning at all costs became his compelling purpose and his downfall as a public figure who was once held in high esteem. His story also reminds us that it's all too easy to lose track of why you play the game. Bold action is essential to moving forward in your drive to live passionately and fully engaged.

CHECKING IN

The Sustainability square, like the Assess square, is on the board as a check-in station where you should pause on a regular basis to make sure that you're playing the game wisely and with a long-term view. Winning at all costs is a very seductive comfort zone, because it obliterates any gray areas. It becomes either win or lose. How you play the game no longer matters—until it does, as attested by Lance Armstrong's tragic example. Seven Tour de France victories mean nothing now, because he played his game from goal to goal instead of from the perspective of sustaining a life's work.

My advice is to play your bigger game while keeping in mind the legacy you'll leave behind. Will your game endure? Will you come to the end still fully engaged and passionate but also proud of how you played and grateful for the life you've led? When you're driven by a compelling purpose, it's not easy to look up and focus that far ahead. I'm guilty of going into survival mode from time to time. Most people are.

We just get so darned busy, caught up in the day-to-day, overwhelmed and overworked. We don't want to take a break for fear of losing momentum or falling behind. But the truth is that we need breaks. Vacations are vital for recharging and reflection, and so are daily workouts. Study after study has shown that increasing our heart rates for even just 30 minutes a day can keep us physically healthier and mentally sharper over the long run.

Personal sustainability encompasses those workout sessions on your own or with a trainer. Meditation, social interaction, supportive and loving relationships, sufficient sleep, regular medical and dental checkups, and ample doses of play—in whatever form most engages you—are also important to sustaining your bigger game and you.

Even companies known for tough bottom-line mentalities have begun to recognize this and take action accordingly. Walmart and Sam's Club, for example, have implemented a costly "personal sustainability" program, estimated to be a $30 million expense, aimed at improving the health and fitness of their workforce, which has been found to have higher rates of heart disease and diabetes than the general public. The program also encourages "green" practices, such as carpooling, waste reduction, the use of nontoxic cleaning supplies, recycling, and decreasing demand on the power grid. Walmart officials weren't sure their employees would embrace the voluntary programs, but to their surprise more than half signed up in the first few months.

THE WHEEL OF LIFE

Here's a handy tool for checking on your sustainability efforts in each of the major areas of your life: career, money, personal development and education, romance, friends and family, health, physical environment, and fun and recreation. My friends at The Coaches Training Institute, where I'm a senior trainer, developed the Wheel of Life, so we thank them for this tool.

Wheel of Life

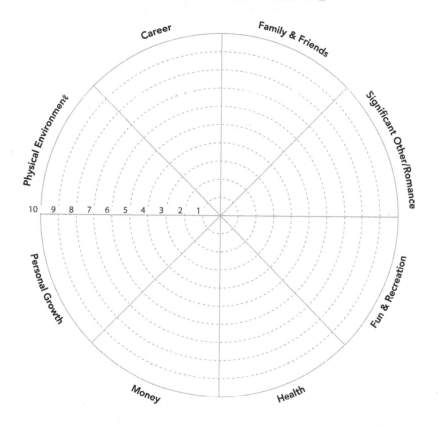

Look at each slice of life in the Wheel of Life above, and on a separate piece of paper grade yourself on a scale of 1 to 10 concerning how you're doing in sustaining yourself there. Be honest (brutally honest, if necessary)! Then look at those areas where you gave yourself a low score and consider what you can do to sustain yourself better.

One of the keys to staying in the game and keeping yourself going is sustaining a high level of passion and commitment. Every day ask yourself where you are in your game, and look at your level of passion for it. If the thrill is gone, maybe you need to up your game or find another one altogether.

THE SUSTAINABILITY PARADOX

You may have already picked up on the Sustainability paradox, which stems from the fact that taking care of yourself is critical because you're the engine that drives your bigger game, but your bigger game must also be set up so that it can survive you. I wouldn't wish for anyone to take a fall like Lance Armstrong, whether he deserved it or not. You may choose to turn your current bigger game over to someone else so you can move on to the next one. Or you may have to bail out for health reasons or simply to move into a perfectly cozy comfort zone for the remainder of your days.

If you want one or more of your bigger games to continue without you, then I'd suggest looking at whether it has what it needs as far as sustainable finances, staffing, leadership, and other key components. One of my favorite examples of a compelling bigger game is MADD, which offers a great example of sustainability put into practice by evolution and adaption. You're probably familiar with this respected organization, but perhaps not yet aware that it was started in 1980 by California mother Candy Lightner after her 13-year-old daughter, Cari, was struck and killed by a hit-and-run driver.

When she learned that the person behind the wheel of the car had an extensive record for driving while intoxicated, Candy became outraged that he was still on the road. With that compelling purpose, she recruited allies and organized Mothers Against Drunk Drivers (MADD) to lobby for greater enforcement and harsher penalties, assist victims and families of those injured by drunk drivers, and increase public awareness of the dangers posed by drivers who've been drinking or using drugs.

For the first few years, Lightner was the face and voice of her organization, and she was highly effective in those roles. She testified, lobbied, and gave speeches and interviews to further her cause. MADD became recognized around the world for its advocacy and effectiveness. Then, after five years, she left MADD to move on with her life. The organization she'd started in her bedroom has continued without her, thanks to the effort she and others put in to making sure it could be sustained. Slightly renamed Mothers Against Drunk Driving, the organization has continued without its founder thanks, in large part, to 600 local chapters across the country operated by activists and advocates who share Lightner's compelling purpose.

Even though MADD has enjoyed strong support from major corporations over the years, donations gathered by its grassroots branches still comprise half of its annual income. Today, MADD has more than two million members and supporters. It's mission has grown to include preventive programs that educate young people about the dangers of drugs and drinking, as well as relentless lobbying for better laws, tougher enforcement, and stiffer penalties.

MADD has done an incredible job of sustaining its efforts for decades, even without its founder. What do you need to do to make sure both you and your bigger game are around for the long haul? What do you need to do to be on top of your game? Do you need to bring in allies whose skills complement and enhance your own? Do you need to take advanced courses in management, finance, or your chosen field? Do you need to bring in partners or investors? Are your marketing and research and development all they need to be?

IMPORTANT, NOT URGENT

As a business owner, I'm aware that asking those questions isn't always a priority. My work requires nearly constant travel and a lot of last-minute scrambling to get where I'm supposed to be in far corners across the globe. Most of us don't have much downtime to reflect on where we are and how to sustain our businesses and ourselves. I'm often guilty of procrastinating, which is one of the most enticing of all comfort zones. I mean, why put off till tomorrow what you can put off for a month—or two or three? As television-advice guru and author Dr. Phil McGraw says, "Someday is not a date."

Many businesses, especially corporations, operate with quarterly goals and deadlines that tend to reinforce short-term scrambling instead of long-term planning. The late personal and career-management advisor Stephen Covey identified four levels of prioritizing for those of us who lean more toward procrastinating. These levels were as follows:

1. Important and urgent

2. Important and not urgent

3. Not important and urgent

4. Not important and not urgent

In his view, important and urgent actions are those that make individuals—and organizations—successful. He contended, and I agree, that too often matters that are "urgent" are usually emergencies that demand immediate attention but take us away from doing things that may be more important over the long term. For example, I may rush to the doctor when bronchitis shuts down my ability to be an effective coach and speaker, but I'll put off having a full physical for as long as I can, even though it may be much more important to my long-term health.

Now if something is both important and urgent, then it does demand our full attention. The problem is that taking the long view and planning for the future are generally regarded as important but not urgent. Global warming is a good example here, unless you're one of the doubters. Although scientists have been telling us for decades about climate change, we had to see polar glaciers melting and rising ocean levels on our shores before our leaders began addressing it.

For most of us, planning for the long term is usually put off until our urgent to-dos are done. You can see ample evidence of this at your local post office at tax-filing time each year as so many people scramble to get their returns mailed by the deadline. You can bet that most of those frantic filers put off the important duty of preparing their tax returns because they had to do more pressing things, like helping the panicked kids with their homework, staying late at the office to meet a deadline, or painting the bedroom before the in-laws arrived.

You're busy. I get it. We're all busy. We all fall into the trap of putting off the tax return or the retirement plan or the annual physical with the procrastinator's mantra, "I'll take care of it later, when I have more time." Unfortunately, this is all too similar to the familiar sign posted in neighborhood bars across the country: "Free beer . . . tomorrow."

Each new day brings urgent tasks and emergencies that kick the can labeled "Important" farther and farther ahead on the calendar of things to do—someday. The remedy for this is the Sustainability square, your place on The Bigger Game Board for putting aside daily distractions. As you step onto this square, keep this mantra in mind: "My legacy depends on taking the long view."

●　✖　●

ASSESSING YOUR GAME ON THE GO

One of my clients, whom we'll call Sue, was the wife of a celebrity and philanthropist, a talented and accomplished man. Sue had been a high achiever in her own career before she and her husband started a family. She came to me for coaching after having three children in just four years. Sue said she loved her husband and kids, but she felt the need for something more.

When I introduced Sue to The Bigger Game Board, she first went to the Assess square. The focus for this square is to dispassionately assess where you are, either as you begin playing your bigger game or while playing the game step-by-step, square by square.

Once you're engaged in your bigger game, you'll likely find yourself returning to this square frequently to gauge where you are and to see what might be needed next. Sometimes you may find yourself standing on the Assess square and one or two other squares at the same time. That's where The Bigger Game meets the game of Twister! So you'll have to be flexible—and focused.

The Assess square is almost always in play, even if you park there just briefly to look at what's true in the present moment. You normally won't spend a lot of time on this spot, but you'll come back to it from other squares or while on other squares, to look at how you're doing and where you need to go next.

If you're just starting out, this is the square for assessing where you are and where you want your bigger game to take you. If you're already engaged in a bigger game, this is the place for looking at how it's going, how you're feeling about it, and where you want to be next on the game board.

It might help to think of this square on The Bigger Game Board as your personal GPS, similar to that on your car's navigation screen or on your smartphone. But instead of being a "global positioning system," this is your "game positioning system." How's your game going? What's needed now? Where are you in your plan to create and play your bigger game?

From this square, you assess not only where you are in relation to "the field" or the world around you, but also where you are in relation to the person you want to be. How excited are you with your life, your present situation, or your current bigger game? Are you having fun yet? Is fun in your future? What impact are you having? How is your bigger game or lack of a bigger game affecting your relationships with family members, friends, and co-workers?

All of these factors are part of the assessment process, because if you aren't receiving payoffs from playing this game, you most likely won't stay with it. Constant assessment and adjustments are necessary, because the real-life "field" you're playing on is constantly changing.

It's similar to the mental processes you go through, often subconsciously, as you drive down the highway. You're always assessing a complex set of factors, including the speed of your car, the distance between your vehicle and those all around you, where you are in relation to your destination, and your car's position on the road in relation to the white lines. Then you have a multitude of other factors that include the weather conditions, position of the sun, and, of course, the text messages coming in on your smartphone (please don't text and drive). It's almost overwhelming to contemplate, but we have the remarkable ability to point ourselves in the right direction and arrive safely.

DOING AND BEING

This book, along with the growth and expansion of The Bigger Game itself, is the result of all the time I spend on the Assess square and in that mode. When I returned to speaking on The Bigger Game after Laura's passing, my compelling purpose was to have millions of people experience the benefits of the concept we'd created. As I played my inner bigger game to figure out how to make that happen, I was constantly assessing where I was and where I needed to go.

If this is my game, what do I need to create? How do I make this a sustainable, far-reaching bigger game?

Now, there are two sides to assessment. There's the *doing* side, which assesses action and the state of your game, and then there's the *being* side, which assesses your physical, mental, emotional, and spiritual state of being as a player.

The doing side is about taking action, and it carries thoughts such as *How do I make this work? Is it working?* and *How can it work better?* Or this form of assessment can ask, *Do I need to take a vacation and give my brain and body a rest?*

The being side involves assessing what your perspective is at any given moment. *Am I fully engaged? Is this still a compelling purpose for me? Do I need to recharge or look elsewhere?*

In my doing assessments, which included discussions with friends and advisors, I realized that in order to generate income and outcomes I needed to design workshops for corporate groups and organizations. Since cloning isn't yet an option—and I'm not sure there's room on this planet for more me—I also needed to train others to run the workshops around the world. I envisioned a small army of allies who could expand my bigger game exponentially to keep it sustainable. Believe me, that wasn't accomplished overnight, but at this point, we've trained more than 75 leaders in the United States, Canada, Australia, Israel, the United Kingdom, South Korea, and Japan.

FEEDING ON FEEDBACK

Another important aspect of the process you engage in on the Assess square is soliciting feedback and assessing it. At the end of every The Bigger Game workshop, we solicit feedback in conversations and in writing. We also encourage participants to stay in touch and offer their later thoughts via e-mail. I'm always making adjustments based on these comments. Sometimes it's not easy to hear if a participant is critical or feels shortchanged. I find myself fleeing to the infamous comfort zones known as "I don't want to hear it!" or "That doesn't make sense."

When harsh criticisms or complaints come in (very rare occurrences, I assure you!), I have to do a "being side" assessment and tell myself to not take it personally and not judge the source, but instead to learn from it and use the criticisms or complaints as motivation to remain compelled and innovative.

One of the constant comments we heard from the beginning was that we needed to do a book that put the players on the board where the rubber meets the road: a new *Play Your Bigger Game* book. Imagine that? A few years ago, I took that feedback into a "doing side" assessment and came to a conclusion that's very often reached on the good ol' Assess square. Laura and I had written a self-published book called *The Bigger Game* with the help of our dear friend Caroline Hall. I knew it was time to go bigger by writing a new book and having it published by an international publisher. Why not dream big, eh?

PUTTING OUT THE CALL

The result of my thoughtful, analytical, nonjudgmental assessment was this: "I need help!" Asking for help is really hard for most of us. Actually accepting it can be equally difficult, because we tend to think that we should be able to do everything ourselves. Maybe that's not true for you, but it certainly is for me. I find it very humbling to admit that I don't know how to do this. You'd think I'd get used to it, because the truth is, the amount of things I don't know how to do is quite large.

After doing that assessment, I stepped over to Bold Action and used a lifeline call to Adora English, who, aside from having a wondrous Dickensian name, is a wondrous connector and networker and get-'er-done sort of person. A former L.A. television producer who now serves as a media-savvy consultant, Adora had been urging me for years to write a guidebook for Bigger Game players.

"I'm ready to take The Bigger Game to the world," I told her.

"I've been waiting years for this call," said Adora, the implorer.

That was a huge assess-ally moment. Actually I was all over the game board, straddling those two squares plus the big *Gulp,* Bold Action, Sustainability—well, if this had been a game of Twister, my body parts would've been severely taxed to hit all the bases.

The fear of asking for help is really silly and self-defeating. We get so wrapped up in not wanting to look silly that we actually do something stupid—we give up. In a blunt and honest assessment, I'd have to ask how a guy who travels the world offering help to others could be afraid to ask for it himself. You see, it turns out that there are many people out there whose mission it is to assist would-be authors in moving past the "would-be" state.

Like many mortals, I'd developed this "story" that I didn't have a book in me: "I'm a much better speaker than a writer. What major publisher would want my book?" I stayed with that self-limiting story, even though my friends and allies were encouraging me to create an inspirational guide for playing The Bigger Game.

The lesson here is to tell the truth to your allies even if you won't accept it for yourself. In my heart of hearts, I knew this new book needed to be expressed; I was just afraid to admit that I didn't know how to do it. But a huge part of playing The Bigger Game is accepting that you don't need the *how;* the game will take care of that.

THE STORIES WE TELL

Our success in reaching our dreams and destinations, despite all of the complexities and distractions we may encounter, is due to a large degree to our ability to constantly assess and adjust. This holds true in our personal lives and our work. In this time of rapidly changing technologies, ever-shifting economic environments, and societal upheaval around the globe, the ability to make fact-based self-assessments by putting judgments aside is critical.

Let's get back to the story of my client Sue. While on the Assess square as a beginner, she stepped out of her wife-and-mother role. She looked at where she was and who she was in relation to where and who she wanted to be. She evaluated her needs and desires for engagement, passion, fulfillment, and fun.

I encouraged Sue not to judge herself for looking beyond the roles of wife and mother, but to look at who she wanted to be and the mark she wanted to make. You want to examine the stripped-down reality of your situation, without critiquing yourself.

We tend to concoct fictions and stories about our lives that affect our perceptions and our actions. Common stories include "I'm not good enough," "I'm a victim," or "My needs aren't a priority." We all develop filters through which we see reality according to past experiences, prejudices, and influences, both conscious and unconscious, but there are ways to get a clear picture despite those filters. We also tend to make judgments that can affect our perception while making assessments, including self-judgment, but again, there are ways to assess reality without declaring who or what is right or wrong.

LEFT-BRAINING IT

The Assess square is for "left-braining" it. The left side of the brain is widely thought to be the primary analytical side of the brain, where certified public accountants, budget analysts, and other bow-tie wearing types are tapped in. Thank God for these folks—I wouldn't be where I am today without my strong left-brain allies. Unlike the artsy right side of the brain, it's all about the facts in this lobe locale.

From your clear-eyed, clearheaded vantage point on the Assess square, you can look out over the rest of the game board and ask (as an individual or as a team) how comfortable you are, how compelled you are, what your hunger level is, and so on. Sue was like many first-time players in deciding to start her first visit to The Bigger Game Board on the Assess square. This location offers an invitation to take the long view, to pause and ask, "Where am I? How am I doing? What am I feeling?"

Sue took time on this square to assess her relationships, her career aspirations, her emotional state, her view of the future, and her perceptions of the past. I can't reveal too much because of confidentiality concerns, but Sue is now off and running on her own bigger game— still happily married, still a devoted mom, but also finding fulfillment in her own endeavors. You won't be surprised to learn that her compelling purpose is to help and encourage other women to make their marks outside of marriage and motherhood.

NOT A VOTE

When you assess something, you do it from a neutral perspective. You aren't voting on it or attaching a judgment to it, because that clouds your vision. It turns your attention from the big picture, the field, to the smaller picture of just yourself. When you're playing your bigger game, you should be constantly assessing without voting or judging. Assessing is gathering the facts. Judging is reaching a conclusion based not just on the facts but emotions, biases, perceptions, and other factors.

You have to have a clear picture of what *is* before you can make a wise decision on what's *next*. As you play your bigger game, you'll need to constantly be assessing the playing field, just as a great quarterback or soccer player is said to have great "field vision." The questions you ask are as follows: "How's the game going?" "Where am I on the timeline?" "What's needed now?" and "Where am I according to the overall plan?"

Again, you do all of this without judgment. You may be familiar with the regional U.S. government office of county assessor. This position, sometimes known as the county tax assessor, is responsible for determining the value of your home and property for purposes of taxation. The county assessor who brings judgment into his work won't likely last long. For example, there's no room for a county assessor to take the following position: "Well, this home must be taxed at a higher rate than a standard three-bedroom, two-bath ranch house because of the beautiful flowers in the front yard and the nice trees in the backyard, and because the guy who owns it is mean to his neighbors."

Can you imagine the outrage if that sort of judgment showed up on the owner's tax bill? The Bigger Game player on the Assess square must be as neutral and dispassionate as the county assessor. It's not as if you were a judge on *The X Factor* or *The Voice*, where you must also take into consideration your rivalry with other judges, the contestant's back story, or Simon Cowell's ire. You deal with just the facts.

STAY OPEN TO THE POSSIBILITIES

I often tell our players that assessing opens up possibilities, while voting or judging tends to limit them. When you can assess dispassionately, you increase your opportunities for flexibility, creativity, and adeptness. However, there's one element beyond the realm of cold, hard truths that I would encourage you to hold on to and use freely on every square and in every aspect of your bigger game: hope—a feeling and an expectation that something positive will happen.

My sister-in-law Betsy taught me that hope can be a critical part of any assessment. She married my brother Keith just a year after he survived an often-deadly heart condition. But It turned out that his battle wasn't over.

Five years into their marriage, and just 14 months after the birth of their daughter, Keith was diagnosed with cancer. It was a rare and particularly deadly form: neuroblastoma. Usually found in children under the age of two, it's known to be especially resistant to treatment in adults.

I've noted that sometimes we choose our bigger games, and sometimes they choose us. Upon learning of Keith's diagnosis, Betsy's bigger game was to help her husband survive. She learned all she could about this form of cancer. One of the most striking facts was that there were fewer than a dozen known cases in the world of this type of neuro-blastoma striking adults. None of those patients had survived.

Betsy made note of that stunning fact and other scary information about the lethal disease. Keith's physician did the same. Doctors are professionally bound to deal with the science. Some are better at doing that than others. There's a balance in which a physician can empathize with the emotions of patients and their loved ones, but the facts must always prevail. Keith was lucky to have a great doctor who fought for him.

Because of the deadly effects of neuroblastoma on adults, most hospitals have no protocol for treating them. Children's hospitals that do treat that cancer in young patients are often unwilling to take adult patients who have it, because they're such a threat to their success rates. Keith was told by doctors at a famous New York City hospital that he had little chance for survival. "We can't do anything for you. Please go home and get your life in order." This terrible news came on a Christmas Eve that I'll never forget.

Despite that, Keith's doctor convinced a children's hospital in Philadelphia to treat him. By the time he entered the six-day treatment program, my brother weighed only 130 pounds and was crippled with pain from tumors on his spine. The treatment was highly aggressive. Betsy likened it to "chemical and nuclear war" on the cancer in her husband's body.

That was her "just the facts" assessment, and it was shared by Keith's doctor, who was equally straightforward in her phone call to Betsy prior to the treatments.

She said, "I think you should know that even if Keith survives the treatment, the tumor will most likely come back."

The doctor cited statistics that underscored her assessment. The data was indisputable, she said.

Betsy was grateful for all this doctor had done for Keith. The physician had championed his cause and fought against tremendous resistance to get him treatment. Betsy could accept that as a medical professional, this doctor had to be straightforward and present the facts based on science. But my sister-in-law refused to accept that assessment if it came without hope.

Why play this cruel and painful game if there's no hope, she thought.

Betsy made her own assessment, and then I think it's safe to say that she moved to the Bold Action square (which just happens to be the subject of our next chapter). After asking a friend to come and be with her husband and daughter at home, Betsy drove into the city and to the hospital where Keith's doctor worked. She waited for hours before finally meeting with her.

"I came here to say that I don't want you to be Keith's doctor anymore," my sister-in-law explained. "I understand completely what you said about his illness and his prognosis. I know how bad this is. I'm not ignorant about the facts. But I can't have a doctor overseeing his care who doesn't believe that he could get well. I just need to have hope. I just need you to believe that it's possible. I don't want you as his doctor if you can't."

After Keith's doctor reported that the cancer would likely return even if this treatment worked, Betsy had reevaluated her bigger game of helping my brother survive. She decided that hope was a key element and that if Keith's doctor didn't have it, then they'd find another physician.

Betsy saw this doctor as her husband's most critical ally. She needed her to buy into Keith's eventual victory over cancer. Betsy was so compelled by her purpose that she convinced the doctor that professional dispassion wasn't enough in this case.

The doctor thought about it and agreed.

"I'll hope with you," the doctor told Betsy.

My brother survived. More than 30 years later, he's senior pastor at the New Hackensack Reformed Church in Wappingers Falls, New York, where he plays his own bigger game, one that he often assesses, always with hope as part of the process.

● ✖ ●

BOLD ACTION PUTS YOUR GAME IN PLAY

Louie Psihoyos (rhymes with sequoias) grew up in Dubuque, Iowa, the quintessential midwestern town on the Mississippi River. Some may think of his hometown as a backwater or flyover, where few people go and many never leave, but Louie disproves that clichéd image and then some.

From an early age, he was driven to act boldly, and his bold actions have taken him around the world many times. Louie had a passion for art and photography even as a boy. He entered and won several Kodak photography contests as a teenager and landed a summer job at his hometown newspaper as a photo intern.

One of the biggest, and strangest, events ever to happen in his hometown occurred while Louie was working at that newspaper during summer vacation from college: Hollywood came to Dubuque. Director Norman Jewison brought actors Sylvester Stallone, Rod Steiger, and the rest of his cast and crew to make the Depression-era film

F.I.S.T. in Dubuque, because it looked more like the time and place of the movie—1930s Cleveland—than did Cleveland itself.

Naturally the newspaper wanted to record the entire filmmaking process, but reporters and photographers were banned from the set. Some of Louie's friends had been hired as extras for the movie, so he sneaked onto the set dressed like them, hiding his camera inside his coat. Some days he hid on rooftops to photograph the day's filming.

On the day that Stallone was to fly into Dubuque, Louie staked out his hotel. The actor arrived from the airport dressed in costume, and Louie took a shot of him standing in the elevator. Stallone loved the photo. The Hollywood star and the kid from Dubuque became fast friends.

To the chagrin of the studio bigwigs, Stallone not only invited Louie to stay on the set, but also gave him a role in the movie as a wedding photographer with one line: "Smile now!" The friendships Louie formed with the Hollywood crowd would last for many years and serve him well.

That wouldn't be the last bold action for this strapping young man from Dubuque. After college, Louie worked for the *Los Angeles Times* and other newspapers before landing a coveted job as a photographer for *National Geographic.* For 18 years, he traveled the globe on assignments for that magazine and others, photographing in beautiful, exotic, and sometimes dangerous locations. He earned a reputation as one of the world's best photographers and later became a sought-after freelance photographer for leading magazines and publications.

Then Louie was compelled to take another bold action and pursue a bigger game. An avid technical diver and conservationist, he'd long been concerned with marine life and the health of the world's oceans. He, along with Netscape founder Jim Clark, a fellow scuba-diving enthusiast, co-founded the Oceanic Preservation Society in 2005 to promote marine conservation and environmentalism. Then, in 2008, Louie joined forces with dolphin activist Ric O'Barry to make a film exposing the annual dolphin capture and slaughter in the seaside town of Taiji, Japan.

Their widely praised 2009 film exposé, *The Cove,* won 25 major documentary film awards, including an Academy Award, bringing worldwide condemnation upon the slaughter of dolphins.

"I consider a film to be a weapon of mass *construction,*" he told an interviewer. "We're not trying to make a movie; we're trying to start a movement to change the way people think about the environment."

Psihoyos continues to lead that movement with his next bold move, an eco-thriller with the working title *The Singing Planet.* This movie, filmed underwater and around the globe, deals with the threat of mass extinctions of species, the rise of toxins in the ocean, and the disappearance of coral reefs.

LIGHTS, CAMERA, ACTION

Louie is the epitome of a natural bigger game player and one of the boldest I've heard of. This chapter looks at the game board's center square, Bold Action, which is in that location because it's a major force behind every bigger game and, for the most part, behind every move you make as a player. It's at the center of the game board because it partners with every other element to move your game forward. And quite frankly, without bold action, it's all just a nice conversation.

When playing your own bigger game as an individual or team member, you'll often be asked to take bold actions to move you out of a comfort zone, to feed your hunger for something more, and to advance your compelling purpose.

Upon first encountering the Bold Action square in The Bigger Game workshops, some participants take on that deer-in-the-headlights expression. The first time they step onto that square, some players' knees shake as if they were standing on the edge of the Grand Canyon. But others find it exhilarating, because once you are on this square, you're not just talking pie-in-the-sky theory; it's no longer about wanting to play a bigger game or hoping to play a bigger game. When you step onto this square, the game is on.

NO HOPE, ALL ACTION

My partner Chuck and I joined thousands of others in an annual California AIDSRide bike ride from San Francisco to Los Angeles several years ago. Each rider recruits donors, who agree to pay a certain amount per mile. It's an incredible event, because you ride down the coast without much fanfare for five days, with little rest and few chances to shower before entering Los Angeles with the streets blocked off and tens of thousands of people cheering. When we arrived weary and dirty, but exhilarated, the founder of the event, Dan Pallotta, a deeply committed Bigger Game player, gave a congratulatory speech, but his opening line threw everyone off.

"There is no hope!" he said.

No hope? Are you kidding me? I did this entire ride, and now at the end, this guy is saying there's no hope. What is up with that?

After such a joyful finish to this ride for a great cause, everyone in the crowd was shocked. But Dan was toying with us.

After saying that there was no hope, he paused to let the thought sink in, and then noted that instead of hope, "There was now $7.6 million in the bank raised by you all for AIDS research and support!"

The crowd then went bonkers, cheering and celebrating. I love the idea of replacing hope with action that brings results. We often have hope that things will change or that we'll make a difference, but through bold action and a bigger game, we can replace hope with actual results. Hope is a wish or a promise. In the case of my brother and my sister-in-law, hope can be a beautiful force. It may also become a comfort zone that can serve you well for a while, until it doesn't. It's one thing to have hope; it's another to take bold action and create a bigger game where there was once just hope. How many of us have this internal voice saying, "I wish this would be different," or "I hope this works out."

The Bold Action square is where you go to close the gap between the way things are and the way you want things to be. It's also the exit zone from your comfort zone. Unless you are an X Games adrenaline junkie, you probably don't equate boldness with comfort. This square is not built for comfort. It's built for speed, and it takes you from 0 to 60, or 160, in just one move. The risks can be calculated, but the rewards will likely exceed the power of your imagination.

Look back at Louie for a second. Can you imagine what a wonderful comfort zone it must have been to enjoy global recognition as one of the best photographers on the planet? How easy would it be to just ride that reputation, travel the world on assignment for *National Geographic* and other esteemed publications, and reap the rewards of his talents and experience?

Yet as high as Louie had climbed—from the rooftops of Dubuque to the summit of his profession and into the upper realms of filmmaking—he keeps reaching for a higher place and a bigger game. His award-winning documentary brought global attention to the massacre of dolphins for the creation of potentially toxic meals. Already, he's moved on to yet another bigger game: to inform and educate his worldwide audience about the destruction of marine life and its impact on the planet.

Louie stepped way out of his comfort zone as a photographer by putting down his still cameras and picking up film and video cameras to make *The Cove*. He and others risked their reputations and even their lives in capturing the underwater footage.

Psihoyos could have cruised in the comfort zone of being a highly respected *National Geographic* photographer, but his compelling purpose drove him to take bold action despite the risks. There's always this element involved in taking bold action, so you'll have to embrace the power of failure as a learning tool.

This square is at the center of The Bigger Game Board, because without bold action, your game will go nowhere. It's also true that every bigger game involves some level of risk and an equal or greater level of boldness. In fact, no matter where you stand on the game board, courage and bold action will come in handy. The origin of the word *courage* means "heart." So doing a bold action from your heart can only serve you—without a doubt.

You step onto this center square when you are ready—or should be ready—to take the leap from contemplating to acting. Looking before you leap is optional. Safety nets are not required. Parachutes are not provided. That's why it's called "bold" action, my friends! I love that classic phrase "Leap and the net will appear."

The Roman poet Virgil said, "Fortune favors the bold." Bigger games favor boldness, too. Even when you don't know what the best move is, you'll be protected in taking a bold action because you have a compelling purpose. If one action doesn't work, that purpose will drive you to keep trying because you're so compelled by the hunger within.

BUILDING "BOLD-MENTUM"

Sometimes we take cover from pursuing our bigger games by clinging to the comfort zone of "I'm in the planning stages" or "I'm working out the details." When you prepare to take a bold action, you don't need to know exactly where it will lead; you aren't required to know exactly where you're headed or how you'll get there. Trust that once you make the leap through bold action, your bigger game will be jump-started and your creativity will help you find your way around obstacles.

Bold action creates a powerful momentum that carries you out of comfort zones and beyond your fear of failure. Bigger game players quickly learn that a failure doesn't mean the end. In fact, failure, setbacks, and obstacles can inspire ingenuity and even genius. You may know that great quote from Winston Churchill: "Success is the ability to move from failure to failure with no loss of enthusiasm."

That's exactly what occurred when local police officers set up blockades and Japanese officials did everything they could to stop Louie Psihoyos and his film crew from having their cameras in the cove during the dolphin slaughter. To get around the opposition's roadblocks, the documentary makers reached out to creative allies, including Industrial Light & Magic, the special-effects company founded by director George Lucas, to craft fake rocks that could be placed underwater with high-definition cameras and microphones hidden inside. They also mounted film cameras on unmanned drones and a small blimp that were flown over the cove by remote control.

Once they had all of the footage they needed, Psihoyos realized that he needed help editing it into a compelling movie, so he brought in another diving buddy, the actor and director Fisher Stevens, who helped craft a strong narrative that gave the documentary the feel of an action thriller and greatly expanded its audience.

Bold action carries you to places beyond your limitations and doubts, attracting allies drawn by your purpose and passion. When you dive headfirst into your bigger game, it takes your attention off nagging doubts, conflicted feelings, and insecurities. It focuses you instead on the playing field, engaging your body, mind, and spirit.

As a serial fretter, I'm a great one for waking up in the middle of the night in a cold sweat, because some previously small concern suddenly looms large over my bed like a monster that's come to devour me. I still have moments of angst when I suffer paralysis by analysis, but I've learned to embrace bold action as the antidote to that.

One of my most recent bold actions was to create and schedule our first Bigger Game Expo. We felt it was time to throw a new piece of spaghetti against the wall to see if it would stick. We had workshops, seminars, and keynote-speaking engagements lined up. But we're not just promoters, we're players, too, so we stepped onto the Bold Action square and said, "What big step forward can we take to advance this bigger game in the world?"

The Bigger Game Expo is designed to showcase inspiring bigger game players, speakers, influencers, and global participants who share ideas, resources, and personal experiences in a retreat environment. For our first one, in May 2013, we had a total of 17 inspiring presenters, including global activist and veteran fund-raiser Lynne Twist, author of the bestseller *The Soul of Money,* and Lucid Living founder Leza Danly, whom I mentioned earlier.

At the expo I had the pleasure of introducing Alice Coles as the recipient of our first Laura Whitworth Bigger Game Player Award. This inspiring lady wowed everyone with her insights and wisdom. These 17 serious players offered fresh perspectives and inspiration for changing the way we look at our relationships with careers, family members, communities, the world, and, equally important, ourselves. Our first conference drew folks from North America, Canada,

Japan, South Korea, Australia, Europe, and the Middle East who are Bigger Game players and advocates.

Our expo reflects both a bold action and a new compelling purpose to showcase the bigger games that others are playing globally. One of my newest bigger games is to show the world all the good work that's going on in our world. The expo's tagline is "Good Work, Great World."

Truly this is a *Gulp* bold action we're taking. What I do know is that there's a hunger in our world to showcase good work. The evidence was shown to us by the number of folks who showed up at our first event of this kind. We're constantly inundated with bad news, so it's time to bring attention to good-news stories. This is another compelling purpose that has been added to my own personal-hunger list.

GOING ALL OUT

Creating and staging these much bigger events is a challenge, without a doubt, but that's the point of a bold action. Of course, not every bold action has to be a huge undertaking, although often the results will be far more rewarding and far-reaching than you may anticipate. This is especially true if your compelling purpose matches a strong hunger in the world around you. A simple bold action can be like a spark that lights up and spreads beyond anything you could imagine.

That's what happened when a small-town law-enforcement professional took one very simple bold action in starting a department Facebook page. David Oliver, the police chief of Brimfield, Ohio, decided to launch a Facebook page so that he could communicate directly and instantly with residents. He thought he might be able to reach a following of 500 or so locals, but his bigger game took off thanks to the global reach of social media and his own appeal as a public servant with a sense of humor.

One of his most popular Facebook postings began with the police chief looking out his office window of the police station and spying a suspicious man waving a beer can and standing in the police parking lot. When the chief went out and spoke with the apparently intoxicated individual, the man confided that he was there to meet a prostitute.

This is the conversation the chief reported on the Facebook page:

> Drunk guy: "I have my $20!"
>
> Chief: "Sir . . . do you know you are at a police department?"
>
> Drunk guy: "I am?"
>
> Chief: "See the uniform? The gun belt? The police car?"
>
> Drunk guy: "&*!# . . . now I do. Am I under arrest?"

While many police departments have Facebook pages these days, the Brimfield police chief goes beyond the usual cut-and-dried postings of crime statistics, prevention warnings, scam artists, lost dogs, and burglary alerts.

For example, Chief Oliver often sends out Facebook warnings to local "mopes" who have attracted the attention of his officers:

> Drug use impacts the user, the family, neighbors, and the community. When several communities are impacted, the region suffers . . . and so on. The people at fault for our drug problems are users and sellers. The people who traffic drugs are greedy, lazy, and the biggest part of our problem. Instead of working for an honest wage, they prey on the weak and make money. If you sell drugs here, leave town immediately. We have 3 certified drug dogs and 12 highly trained and very eager officers who are looking for you . . . and their boss gives them all the time, tools, and resources they need . . . Chief.

The uniquely presented Facebook page that Chief Oliver set up has drawn comments from visitors in 19 states and 31 countries and has attracted as many as 1.5 million visitors on weekends. So, I guess you can say that the chief's simple bold action expanded his field of influence from Brimfield to the world!

WELCOMING CHALLENGES

If you're to play a bigger game, you have to commit to constantly challenging yourself. Not committing is another enticing comfort zone, of course, but in my acting days, I learned that you have to go all out as soon as you step onstage or the cameras start rolling. The 2013 Academy Award winner for best actor, Daniel Day-Lewis, a role model for every actor, also strikes me as a great role model for Bigger Game players. There's no doubt that he's another natural, especially when he says things like this: "My ambition for many years was to be involved in work that was utterly compelling to me, regardless of the consequences."

Day-Lewis is one of the most respected of modern-day film actors, and he's known for boldly diving into his roles so deeply that he remains in character throughout the entire production of his movies. He's said that when filming is over, he often grieves the "death" of his character for weeks.

When he portrayed the severely disabled Irish painter and writer Christy Brown for the 1989 movie *My Left Foot,* Day-Lewis remained in a wheelchair and required the cast and crew to feed him throughout filming. He sounded very much like a bigger game player as he described that bold action in an interview: "Playing the part of Christy Brown left me with a sense of setting myself on a course, of trying to achieve something that was utterly out of reach."

To prepare for his role as Hawkeye, the Native American Indian in *The Last of the Mohicans,* he spent days living off the land in an Alabama forest, eating only what he killed and cooked himself.

For his Oscar-winning performance in the 2012 hit *Lincoln,* the actor did intense study to both look and sound like the late president. One reviewer noted, "Plenty of performers can change their accent, posture, or waistline to suit the part. Day-Lewis alone seems capable of remolding his larynx and vocal cords."

It takes boldness and courage to commit to a role like that, because if you miss the mark, you may face criticism. But bold action is about joy, too. This square on The Bigger Game Board is anchored in the principle that life is an adventure to be embraced and experienced with joy and all of the energy you can summon.

That approach to your bigger game and your life will help you take on anything and everything that comes at you. The dynamic power of bold action forces your focus away from self-defeating and debilitating thoughts. When we act boldly, we disarm them of their power. They dissipate in the exhilaration of playing your bigger game. You cease to worry about problems and, instead, focus on creative solutions, such as placing your film cameras in fake rocks, on drones, and in blimps! As the German philosopher Goethe said, "Boldness has genius, power, and magic in it."

TAKE A BOLD ACTION AND CALL ME IN THE MORNING

You might want to think of the Bold Action square as made of Teflon, because you'll never feel *stuck* when you're on it. I noted earlier in the book that playing The Bigger Game means you'll never be stuck again, and that's primarily because you always have the option of taking a bold action that frees you.

You get stuck when you're in a comfort zone, or a discomfort zone, and you can't figure out how to escape. Maybe you're in an uninspiring job and you feel you don't have any other options but to stay. Maybe you're stuck in a relationship that's no longer fulfilling, but you're equally unenthusiastic about breaking up and being alone.

Consider your own situation for a moment. If you're feeling stuck in some aspect of your life right now, what bold action could you take in the next few days to free yourself or at least to open up fresh opportunities? The great thing about this square is that you can take a bold action without knowing what your bigger game is.

My partner, Chuck Lioi, has done this repeatedly, and to his amazement, he has ended up in a game bigger than before after each bold action. After graduating from college with a communications degree, Chuck's dream was to land a job as a small-market television reporter and work his way up to larger stations. He'd picked up a lot of valuable experience working on his college television-station broadcasts, so Chuck thought he had a shot in the real world. But after several station managers told Chuck he looked "too young for television," he assessed his situation and decided to go backstage.

He moved to New York City without a job, but quickly found work as a production manager for corporate media departments. He picked up more experience and then landed a job on the production staff of the soap opera *One Life to Live.* He rose to the rank of associate producer, which was an administrative job, where he dealt with scheduling and budgets and in general kept the show running.

Three years later, a new executive producer joined the show and cleaned house, giving Chuck one job: to leave. He boldly packed up and moved to Los Angeles, again without a job. And again, he quickly found work on television soap operas, talk shows, and pilots in L.A. His goal was to land a prime-time show that lasted for more than a few episodes, but two years in a row, Chuck had shows canceled on the day before Christmas.

He decided it was time to do another assessment of his career choice. He was still weighing his next bold action, when I asked him to join me in growing my executive, personal, and organizational development business and The Bigger Game workshops. Now, this may have been Chuck's most brazen bold move, because it took him out of his television-production comfort zone, but it's worked out to our mutual benefit. Together, we've created a bigger game that keeps us both hopping from one bold action to the next. This is now the Allies square alive and well, for he's what I call a co-player in the same game—we're both in it 100 percent.

BOLD LINKS

The Bold Action square is also one that links quite easily with each of the other squares. If you find yourself on the Sustainability square, for example, you might want to ask, "What's a bold action I can take to better sustain my long-term health?" Some potential bold actions in this realm could include joining Weight Watchers or signing on with a personal trainer, and giving up smoking would definitely be a bold and smart action in the sustainability arena. Personally, a bold action for me in this category is to say no to bread. I'm not kidding. I love bread. Give me cinnamon toast, give me muffins, and give me a BLT on whole wheat with mayo!

Saying no to bread at mealtime is a bold action for me because I love it so much, but the truth is that I feel much better when I eliminate flour from my diet. So if I'm to stand in the Sustainability square, this would be a wise move for me. It's a bold action on a small scale, but it takes me out of my comfort-food comfort zone.

My friend Erin Grayson discovered her compelling purpose as a player of The Bigger Game and has learned to link it with bold action. In fact, she had just put her boldest bold action in play as I was writing this book. Erin is preparing to leave an exceedingly comfortable comfort zone in a job that she earned after years and years of incredibly hard work.

Remarkably, Erin was already a hero to me and many others who know her well. The snapshot of her heroic story is this: Erin, who is 31 years old, has a master's degree even though she can read only on a third-grade level.

"I've never actually read a book," she told me.

Those seemingly contradictory facts can be explained by Erin's unique nature. Since early childhood, she has had to deal with severe dyslexia, but she's been blessed with an extremely bright mind and a deep well of determination. Erin isn't a typical graduate of The Bigger Game workshop either. She's a world-class player, a natural, and probably the leading scholar on the topic, since she wrote her master's thesis on using The Bigger Game as a leadership tool for young adults.

NO LIMITS

A native of Norwich, New York, Erin was diagnosed with dyslexia in the third grade. She had entered school early, at the age of four, because she was so bright. Although she did well in math and science, she struggled from her first reading classes. Her mother, a teacher, detected this early on and became Erin's champion, pushing for her school to have her tested to determine the exact nature of her learning disability.

Before her school finally did that, Erin went through a couple of very challenging years. She comprehended everything that was taught to her verbally and mastered it easily. In fact, when she was finally tested, she scored at the high-school level in her ability to understand and retain information imparted verbally. But it was impossible for her to learn from reading material on her own. She had to leave her classroom for special tutoring during language-arts classes or written tests, which resulted in labeling, teasing, and bullying from other students, who called her "retarded" and "stupid."

"I felt I was too smart to have a learning disability, so I went through this period of feeling broken," Erin told me. "People were always trying to fix me. My response to that was a low level of self-esteem coupled with a strong desire to be perfect in everything I did."

Like many intelligent people with dyslexia, Erin found ways to learn despite the disability. She found herself in the unusual position of having to defend her nomination for the National Honor Society, because some of the faculty argued, "If she's so smart, why does she have to have other people read her schoolbooks to her?"

Some counselors told Erin that she shouldn't plan on going to college. She ignored them. To overcome her disability, she had to learn to become her own best advocate, fighting for study assistance and testing procedures suited to her verbal-learning skills. She learned to use computer programs that allowed her to dictate her papers, and the school provided support staff to read textbooks to her. It took Erin three times as long to write papers and read lessons, but she earned her degree, majoring in youth development and minoring in sociology and music. And then she boldly and bravely announced her next bigger game: graduate school and a master's degree in recreation.

"My undergraduate advisor thought I should just get a job, but I wanted a master's degree, and since school is so hard for me, I was afraid that once I left, I'd never go back," Erin told me. "It wasn't easy, but grad school was incredibly rewarding, even though writing my thesis was hell."

I met Erin while she worked summers during college and grad school at the beautiful 110-year-old Silver Bay YMCA retreat and conference center, where my brother also works. My summer cottage isn't far from Silver Bay, and we use their facilities for many of our workshops, including The Bigger Game Expo conference. Once Erin was introduced to The Bigger Game, she became an avid and expert player. She had benefited a great deal from YMCA leadership programs in high school. Erin was compelled to use The Bigger Game as a tool for developing young leaders, and she even wrote her thesis on it, which was such an honor. After she earned her master's degree, Erin became director of leadership development and family programs at the Silver Bay YMCA.

She loved her job, which included living quarters on the 700-acre Silver Bay campus overlooking Lake George, set in the natural wonderland of Adirondack Park in upstate New York. There, Erin found her career passion and her artistic husband, Tim, a gifted jewelry maker and sculptor.

Since completing grad school in 2006, Erin has been a leader at Silver Bay. In fact, she wrote its leadership-development program. But as an avid bigger game player, she decided in 2012 that she needed to take a bold action. Because of its beautiful surroundings and wonderful working environment, Silver Bay is a high-level, nearly irresistible comfort zone. Yet Erin has decided that her passion for developing young leaders would best be applied on a college campus. Since Tim is also interested in obtaining a master's degree, this amazing couple is now in the process of looking for just the right college or university for the next stage of their bigger games.

"I always refused to stay in comfort zones as a child, and I don't want to be trapped in them as an adult if I feel the need for growth and a larger field," she said. "That's why I'm taking a bold action."

"I have a passion for working with college-age people in transition and helping them find their gifts to share with the world, and I am compelled to do that," Erin said.

My young friend Erin was enjoying a great career and a great life in one of the world's most beautiful settings, yet she had the wisdom to realize that she had a bigger game to play, and the courage to take bold action so that she might fulfill her compelling purpose on a larger field. This incredible and inspiring woman has been overcoming challenges, breaking free of labels, and exceeding expectations all of her life. I may just have to redesign The Bigger Game Board and put her face on the Bold Action square, because as far as I'm concerned, she owns it!

The question to ask yourself is, "What's a bold action I could take today or this week to recharge my life?" It may or may not be related to your bigger game. What matters is that it's something that takes you out of your own comfort zone. Maybe it's to join a gym, pick up the phone and ask for help from a friend, or dare to ask for a raise—whatever it is, know that you're activating the human spirit of creativity and innovation. Just by doing something that's not "business as usual," you'll be inviting into your life a new energy that will build on itself and put something into motion. I dare you to go take one bold action right now, as soon as you finish reading this chapter.

● ✖ ●

AFTERWORD

YOUR GAME
MAY FIND YOU

David Gillespie, a firefighter for the city of Peterborough, Ontario, had been searching for some time to find a way "to make a mark on this world." He participated in The Bigger Game workshop in 2010, hoping to find a way to do that.

On the second day of the workshop, conducted by Bigger Game trainers Sue Gleeson and Shannon Kelly, David was working on identifying his compelling purpose, when it dawned on him that he didn't have to search for his bigger game any longer. It had found him. In fact, David's bigger game had come with him to the workshop; he just hadn't realized it was there.

At the end of the first day of our workshops, I give participants homework assignments meant to open their hearts and minds to whatever bigger games are awaiting them. My intent is to raise their antennae and their levels of awareness so they can identify potential bigger games as they dream or ponder the wealth of material presented in that initial day of the workshop.

There are always a few who are already dead-on certain of the bigger games they want to play. But most participants are just feeling the first pangs of hunger for "something more" in their careers, relationships, or daily lives. I don't want anyone to feel pressured. There's no expectation that they come up with a clearly defined game at any point in the workshops—no pressure, no goals.

Many first-time players go into a particular comfort zone at this stage, and some remain there for a long time. It's called the comfort zone of "I need to figure this out."

Too often, they put pressure on themselves, because they feel that they have to "get this right" or identify "the perfect name" for their games during the workshop, or at least by the end of it.

If you find yourself working really, really hard to find your bigger game, you aren't ready. My advice is to let go of that and just be open. This is the spiritual or Zen aspect of The Bigger Game. Don't try to find your game; just be aware and ready for it to find you. Be open, available, and in the creative state of flow—fully engaged and always aware.

Once you understand The Bigger Game philosophy and methodology, trust the process. Hang on to uncertainty and ambiguity and "not knowing." Give yourself permission to be a Bigger Game player in waiting. Understand that you're always on the game board, so don't tear your hair out or feel pressured. You don't have to figure it out right away; just stay in the moment and wait for it. Your bigger game will reveal itself when you're ready for it. That may happen during my workshop, a few days later, or even months or years later.

In David Gillespie's case, when he walked into The Bigger Game workshop, the catalysts for his compelling purpose were with him. David actually had part of it on his mind and another part in his heart.

Mentally, he was very aware of a hunger to make a mark on the world, but he didn't yet know how.

Emotionally, he was carrying the memory of a recent hometown tragedy, one that would resonate with him during the workshop.

Just a few weeks earlier, a four-year-old boy had drowned in a river that runs in front of David's house. Despite the best efforts of the firefighters, they had been unable to revive the boy. Men and women in the rescue business know that they can't save everyone.

Often, they arrive too late to the scene of fires and accidents to help those who've been severely injured. Still, every lost life weighs heavily on those who are so dedicated to saving others.

Although firefighters and rescue-squad members are trained mostly to react to emergency situations, The Bigger Game workshop opened David up to also thinking in proactive terms about his life's work. It struck him that he might be able to satisfy his hunger to "make a mark on the world" by looking at the bigger picture and thinking longer term about the tragedy that had occurred in front of his own home. He defined his compelling purpose, then, as "reducing drownings around the world."

"A drowning is one of the hardest calls to deal with, because it is preventable and [must be resolved in] only a few minutes," he said. "Following the workshop handbook, I took . . . bold action and wrote a successful concept plan to create a YouTube video for drowning prevention."

David did his research and found there was a demand for quality instructional information on water safety that parents could teach their children. He put out calls for allies and investments. He quickly lined up support from local police and fire departments. A partnership of allies was developed among local schools; Peterborough Fire Services; and former Olympic figure skater Barbara Underhill, whose daughter had drowned in a swimming pool.

With his allies, David produced a three-minute safety-instruction video titled "Swim to Survive." The video demonstrates three basic water-survival skills, including how to safely get oriented after falling into deep water, how to tread water, and how to do the dog paddle. The program was set up for parents or teachers to watch on a laptop, computer, or smartphone so they could train others, and the video has been translated into eight languages and viewed around the world on YouTube and other social-networking sites.

"The Bigger Game gave me the tools to move from being reactive as a firefighter to now proactively promoting a hands-on water-safety program," said David.

PATIENCE IS PART OF THE GAME

If you've reached this Afterword with a bigger game firmly in mind, congratulations! In a few more pages, I'll provide you with some thoughts on playing that game and others for the rest of your life.

On the other hand, if you've yet to name your game, I'm excited for you because you're now fully prepared to recognize it when your compelling purpose kicks in. Believe me, if you don't find your bigger game, it will find you!

That's what happened to me. I certainly didn't sit up in bed one morning and say, "My bigger game is to travel the world encouraging people to play The Bigger Game!" No, the material in this book evolved over time, and it came to me through many allies and our shared experiences and ideas. So, I have no expectation that all who take my workshops or hear me speak will immediately identify their compelling purposes and be off and running with their bigger games. I do, however, have intention to activate the desire to become a Bigger Game Player.

People often find that their bigger games develop slowly before they become well-formed concepts. This happened to Faith Anaya, who participated in The Bigger Game workshop in Chicago in 2008. She was new to The Bigger Game Board but not the concept of consciously creating her own life. At that point, Faith had already put her MBA to extensive use for more than 14 years in San Francisco, where she worked 70 hours a week as a logistics consultant on projects of up to $500 million.

By the time we met in Chicago, she'd left her hard-charging corporate career to start a family; raise her son; and launch her own business, Kids Cook!, which is a thriving cooking school for children in Little Rock, Arkansas. During a break in the Chicago workshop, I asked Faith about the hunger that she felt for "something more" and her compelling purpose. At first, she indicated that she was still trying to figure some of that out, but then she said, "I work mostly with kids whose parents can afford to pay for cooking classes, but there are a lot of hungry kids out there who can't even afford to pay for lunch—and I know there must be a way to bring them together."

Faith seemed surprised to hear those words come out of her mouth. I realized that she'd just stated her compelling purpose for the first time. That has been known to happen in The Bigger Game workshops. In fact, one of my most important missions is to create an environment where participants can do that. Still, expressing a compelling purpose and naming a bigger game are two very different steps in the process, and Faith, like many people, didn't find her game quite as quickly as she found her purpose.

After completing the workshop, she returned to Little Rock and pondered what her next bigger game might look like. Several months later, she read an article about a flour company in Vermont that was donating its product to students so they could bake bread for soup kitchens. As you might imagine, that idea resonated with Faith and her compelling purpose. She put out feelers in her own community, and when the holidays rolled around, she found herself leading area students in baking 900 dinner rolls for a local project to provide Christmas meals to needy families.

That successful and joyful undertaking led to the creation of Faith's bigger game, Kids Cookin' for a Cause! Now in its fifth year, her nonprofit has so far enlisted more than 500 young people, ranging from kindergarteners to 12th graders, who have helped produce an estimated 5,000 pounds of food (mostly pasta)—enough to provide 10,000 meals for hungry kids.

One of the rewards of her bigger game is the fact that just a few years into it she's already seeing young people step up and take responsibility for producing the food, which tells Faith that this is a very sustainable game.

"Last December, I did almost nothing other than show up with the ingredients and cook the pasta," she said. "They organized themselves, and boom, boom, boom—they put the meals together. I'm really proud of how hard they've worked and the connection they have with it. I went to The Bigger Game workshop because I wanted my projects to be bigger than [I am], and that has definitely happened. I love that the kids have taken over."

Faith's other favorite lesson from the creation of this bigger game is that "things happen when you are open to the possibilities."

"I tell the young people I work with that often the most authentic ideas come from a lot of openness to possibilities and to just connecting the dots," she said. "Ideas are out there—it is our ability to pay attention that takes something from a nice idea to a bigger game. Kids Cookin' for a Cause grew out of my openness to possibilities."

WORKS IN PROGRESS

Bigger games often take time to reveal themselves to us in much the same way that Michelangelo slowly freed his artistic vision from the material that kept others from seeing it: "In every block of marble I see a statue as plain as though it stood before me, shaped and perfect in attitude and action. I have only to hew away the rough walls that imprison the lovely apparition to reveal it to the other eyes as mine see it."

Some of the best bigger games are those that are slow to reveal themselves. Natural bigger game player Ray Anderson, who passed away in 2011 at the age of 77, found his biggest game late in life and earned global recognition as a champion of the "green" movement in business. He was a late arrival to that movement as well.

In the early 1990s, Anderson was known as "the king of carpet tile." The Georgia Tech grad was founder, chairman, and CEO of Interface, the world's biggest manufacturer of carpet tiles, which are created from petroleum products in a process that was then contributing substantially to the buildup in landfills around the world.

Anderson started Interface in 1973, at a time when carpet tiles were shunned as low-class industrial alternatives to residential carpet sold in rolls. Twenty years later, Interface had 29 manufacturing sites around the world and sales of nearly a billion dollars.

Anderson, whom I met at a leadership conference several years ago, considered himself an entrepreneurial role model until he began taking heat from customers and the growing "green" movement. One of his employees gave him a copy of *The Ecology of Commerce* by Paul Hawken. A successful entrepreneur with a strong social conscience, Hawken was sounding alarms about the destructive environmental impact of manufacturing. He was also calling out businesses to find and promote solutions that made economic and environmental sense.

Ray Anderson often said that reading Hawken's book was like being speared in the chest. He'd always been proud of his company's success and its strong record of following government regulations. But after reading the book, Anderson realized that the environmental impact of his business was every bit as destructive as Hawken claimed.

He admitted to being "a plunderer of the earth." Andersen and his wife cried as they read the book and recognized that his approach to business "was all wrong." To his credit, the king of carpet tile soon became a champion of responsible environmental business and manufacturing. He slowly transformed his own company, enduring sales declines and criticism from shareholders, until it became a model for its efforts to promote sustainability while remaining profitable.

He brought in Hawken as well as other environmental advisors and green-movement pioneers as allies to help him figure out how to make the carpet-manufacturing business more environmentally responsible. In the decades that followed, Interface's stock price rose 70 percent, profits soared by 81 percent, and sales climbed by 77 percent even as the company began using fewer raw materials and cutting emissions and solid waste in its manufacturing processes.

Anderson called his bigger game "Mission Zero," because his goal was that Interface would one day leave no environmental footprint. Because of his green efforts in his business and his frequent speeches on the topic, Anderson became one of the world's leading evangelists for "sustainability as good business." He served as co-chair for President Bill Clinton's Council on Sustainable Development to help create government policy to address global warming. In 2007, *Time* magazine listed the self-described recovering plunderer as one of its "Heroes of the Environment."

Ray Anderson was 64 when the biggest game of his life found him. It changed his life in a very radical way. His Mission Zero program was certainly not business as usual! He spent the last 14 years of his life reminding other business and government leaders, "We are all part of the continuum of humanity and life. We will have lived our brief span and either helped or hurt that continuum and the earth that sustains all life."

There are many inspiring aspects to Ray's story, but I hope one takeaway for you will be that you should always be open to newer bigger games no matter where you are in life. Ray was a very wealthy and respected businessman who easily could have chosen a comfortable retirement. Instead, he followed the bigger game that came to him, one that has had a lasting and profound impact.

BEING, NOT TRYING

It's interesting also that when Ray Anderson's bigger game revealed itself to him, he described it as feeling like "a spear to the chest." I hear similar descriptions from newly minted bigger game players all the time. For some, the "reveal" comes with a rush of joy. For others, it's a kick in the pants. Discomfort can be a major catalyst for change. It's an alarm sounding the call to action.

At the end of the first day of a workshop in Los Angeles, one of the participants came up to me and said she was really struggling with identifying her compelling purpose and hadn't a clue what her bigger game might be. She was uncomfortable with that. I told her that discomfort was a good sign. I advised her to go home, have a nice dinner, and not stress out.

"There's no deadline," I assured her. Deadlines can be a comfort zone for many folks.

Before the next morning's first session, she informed me that her compelling purpose and her bigger game had hit her "like a lightning bolt" while she was driving to the workshop. So for her, the reveal didn't come with a stab to the chest; it was a jolt from a bolt! She was an avid distance runner. Becoming fit had changed her life. She felt compelled to share the benefits of health and exercise with others. Once she'd become comfortable with her discomfort, her hunger and compelling purpose led her to a bigger game.

Fear not! Your Bigger Game is out there in the universe. You'll find each other if you remain open and ready for it to reveal itself. It's not always a personal tragedy or realization that calls you to action, but often that's the case. There's no need to get all bent out of shape in searching—no need for angst. Instead, quiet your mind and feel your emotions. Be still and wait for it.

In recent years, I've been asked to do many workshops in Japan, Korea, and China. What I've found is that this concept of not *trying*, but *being*, is still very much a part of the Zen philosophy and Asian culture. Yet Asians who have moved to the United States and Europe tend to adopt the more aggressive, goal-oriented lifestyles and philosophies of the West.

Now, however, many in the East are yearning to return to a more traditional approach to life. Following the earthquakes and devastating tsunami in Japan, my phone began to ring with calls from a steady stream of former and aspiring clients. Out of this tragedy, opportunities will arise. They're calling me to help them prepare for those bigger games that will surely come for them—as they will for you, too.

This is a no-pressure situation. We play here. We don't plot, demand, or "set the bar." Laura and I originally chose the metaphor of The Bigger Game because when we play, we tap into our highest levels of creativity and engagement. This is about finding your passion and purpose and whatever it is that so fully engages you that it never feels like work.

I don't put pressure on players to name their games. Instead, I encourage them to be open to allowing a bigger game to find them. I say that repeatedly during my workshop and speeches because it works. Those who relax and let their games come to them are often the most compelled and engaged players, because their bigger games are almost like spiritual quests for them.

When you identify a hunger and become clear on your compelling purpose, you're on the path to your bigger game. You'll find that ideas and opportunities present themselves like never before. Circumstances will suddenly shift. People who share or appreciate your passion and purpose will also magically appear to serve as guides, encouragers, and allies. I'm sure you've heard the saying, "When the student is ready, the teacher will appear." It's the same with bigger game players and their games.

HARNESSING THE PASSION

Some of the most avid and compelled bigger game players I've known have been around the same retirement age as Ray Anderson when their games found them. Their examples always serve to remind me that playing The Bigger Game isn't about your age; it's about your compelling purpose, which can be ignited at any point in life. You may not always be able to run 10 miles or lift 100 pounds, but you can always be passionate about those things that matter most to you—and that's what drives your bigger game.

You may not feel like a particularly passionate person, but believe me, it's only a matter of having the right button pushed. At the age of 21, I was caught up in the bigger game of helping my brother Keith in his fight with cancer. This was definitely a game that found me and that changed the way I viewed my life.

There was one night when I stayed with Keith in the hospital. I slept in a bed beside his, and he was in terrible pain. They were giving him cocaine mouthwashes to numb his mouth, because the chemo was peeling the surface of his mouth and tongue. He screamed in pain during the night. Alarmed, I went down the hall and asked the nurse to give him some meds.

"It's not time yet," she said.

I'm sure she didn't mean to seem uncompassionate. She may have had other duties distracting her, or maybe she'd been given strict orders. Whatever her motives, she was about to feel the wrath of one much-more-motivated little brother. I was focused on Keith and his pain, and I wanted him to get relief.

I said, "I know you have rules, but I must tell you, he needs this now. Thank you for doing your work, but he's been in the hospital for weeks and one more cocaine swish isn't going to kill him. He's barely alive now, so give me the damned swish!"

It was the first time in my life I'd felt so strongly about something that I confronted an adult and challenged her. To my surprise, the nurse responded by bringing the pain relief for Keith. I was a little taken aback. I felt like someone who just discovered a superpower.

I can do that? Me?

That was a defining moment in my life; I realized for the first time the power that comes with passion and total commitment.

When you're compelled to play your bigger game, you, too, will break through all inhibitions and self-imposed limitations. Your passion will drive you in ways that inspire others. That's the level of energy generated when you play your bigger game.

My experiences with Keith during his cancer fight gave me my first sense of the power that comes with purpose and passion. That's what should drive you, too, throughout your life, without stopping until you've used up every minute of your allotted time on this earth.

Even better, when I felt compelled to help my brother, I was driven by something outside myself. We've all heard stories of horrible moments when a child is trapped under a car and a mother, sibling, or passerby finds the strength to lift the car. All "common sense" goes out the window when the adrenaline surges and passion flares; that's how you want to feel in your bigger game.

PLAYING FOR LIFE

When you're truly compelled by a desire to make a difference and move beyond business as usual, you become capable of creating and achieving miraculous results. Too often we allow ourselves to be limited in our thinking: *That's the way it's always been, so that's the way it will always be. I can't do that; I don't have that kind of power.*

The key to becoming a lifelong bigger game player is to follow your passion and keep it alive. Too often, people run from passion instead of embracing it. Their bigger games present themselves, but they're unwilling to leave the comfort zone of just trying to survive or working to make ends meet. Some may take tentative steps toward the bigger game that's calling them, but if they don't see a payoff right away, they go scrambling back to the comfort zone.

Bigger games rarely are about short-term gratification. They are long term, and in most cases, constantly evolving. Once you name your game, recruit allies, and take your first bold action, everything is in play, including constant change. You have a vision for your game, and that's good. But remember the Yiddish proverb that says, "Man plans. God laughs." Your game will evolve minute by minute, adjusting to the need in the field, and you'll have to keep a light hand on the wheel. You may find it helpful to keep your compelling purpose on a plaque where you can see it. As your game evolves, you want to make sure it still serves your needs and those of the field.

This is where the Assess square becomes critical to your long-term success as a player on The Bigger Game Board. It's there for you to step onto and ask if your evolving game still supports the change you want to create. "Is my game still big enough to challenge and grow the person I'm becoming? How's my game going? How am I doing? What needs to happen next?"

The long-term player of The Bigger Game has to navigate the ever-changing field, using obstacles as opportunities, allowing your game to evolve and evolving with it, or abandoning it altogether if a new and even bigger game presents itself. It's great to have a plan, but not great to be so attached to it that you miss the point of being in the game. It's not so much a strategic process as it is organic.

Just ask Kathryn Bigelow, who won an Academy Award for best director in 2010 with *The Hurt Locker,* which also won the Oscar for best picture. She followed that critically acclaimed film with another best picture nominee *Zero Dark Thirty* in 2012. But Bigelow had actually been working on a different screenplay and movie after *The Hurt Locker.* She'd just begun work on that movie when Osama bin Laden's hiding place was discovered.

Change of plans! During research for another film, Bigelow had heard of CIA female officers involved in tracking him. She then came up with a new script that put a woman CIA officer at the center of the new film. She definitely adjusted her bigger game in a big way but still followed her compelling purpose of shedding light on the intelligence agencies and their search for their number one target.

When asked about her plans after *Zero Dark Thirty,* the first woman to win an Oscar for her work as a director spoke like a natural-born bigger game player.

She said in a *New Yorker* interview, "Usually what happens is something will reveal itself. And then there will be an urgency, and then I can do nothing else but that."

Playing your bigger game is not about keeping an eye on the prize; it's about constantly assessing and being alert to your compelling purpose.

The driver who keeps his eyes on his GPS system instead of the actual road will certainly crash and burn, and the same is true of the bigger game player who focuses on the plan rather than the field. Your attention should be on how your game plays out, how it's received, and whether it's having the intended impact. Most of all, is it serving your compelling purpose?

I have a timeline for The Bigger Game workshop, but I'd be crazy if I didn't constantly monitor how participants are responding—or not responding—to the material and the concept. The dynamics are different with each group of individuals. Humor plays well with some, not so well with others. Some are very earnest. Others are wildly creative or subversive. My game evolves according to the needs of the field for each session and, over time, their cumulative responses over the years. I have allies who help me assess as I go. Here are some questions I ask myself during my workshops. Feel free to adapt them for your own purposes:

* What happened today? This week? This month? This year?

* What do I need to do better?

* What would engage participants more?

* Where does The Bigger Game concept need to be stronger?

* What new elements have emerged?

* What are participants responding to?

* What seems to resonate with them?

* What helps them the most in identifying and pursuing their own bigger games?

* What tools can I give them for playing their games day in and day out?

I'm always introducing new metaphors and trying out new ideas. Some of them actually work. Many flop. But that's part of the game, too. If you aren't failing now and then, you aren't playing a big enough game. Failures set you up for success, because they force you to evolve and grow with your game. Change is inevitable, but it isn't always necessary. Sometimes, your game will be ticking along like a clock. Be grateful for those stretches, but don't get too comfortable.

Comfort zones aren't inherently good or bad. You know that, but as you play the game over time, you'll see that they form quickly. As soon as you break free of one, you find yourself in another. One behavior pattern is broken only to see another form. Recognize them all and avoid those that make you complacent or dull your senses. Remember, discomfort in the form of a new hunger is often a good indicator that another game is afoot, hopefully a bigger and better game at that!

Your compelling purpose is the North Star, the one aspect that remains your guiding constant, but like Kathryn Bigelow, you can express that compelling purpose in many, many ways and through many different games.

STEP IT UP

You may be surprised to learn that Kathryn Bigelow was a promising painter before she became a filmmaker and director. Her natural tendency to play bigger and bigger games transformed her into something she may never have imagined for herself—she became a leader. When you play your bigger games throughout your life, you take on the role of leader, even if that has never been a goal.

I believe we all qualify as leaders when we make the decision that our lives will make a mark, whether it be on our families, our organizations, our companies, or wherever we're called to. Great bigger game players and great leaders are game changers. It takes courage to step up, just as it does to commit to playing a bigger game. Once you're lit up with a compelling purpose and your bigger game has found a way into your mind, heart, and soul, look out. Get ready for a wild ride!

In early 2013, I was a keynote speaker at the annual Young Presidents' Organization global conference, which was held in Istanbul, Turkey. First of all, what an honor, and second, even five years ago, I would not have imagined myself bringing The Bigger Game message to such a prestigious global leadership organization. Like me, you'll have to learn to receive all the amazing opportunities the world brings to your door when your bigger games unfold on the largest possible stage. I'm deeply grateful, which is a comfort zone that I love to practice daily. Gratitude is a beautiful source for experiencing a full, rich life.

So what I know for you is this: You are worthy of a life even greater than you can imagine. Dare to dream it. Dare to live it. Dare to play your bigger games. If you do that, an extraordinary life awaits.

Now that you know The Bigger Game philosophy and methodology and The Bigger Game Board, you're well on your way. Just by reading this book, you've set in motion something in your life that's bigger than you ever thought possible. Be on the lookout for messages, people, or circumstances that seem to appear out of nowhere. They're your allies!

Be open and prepared for your bigger game to find you. Don't try! Be! Let go and trust the process, for there are already forces in play. Stand ready to be connected to what matters to you, and to experience the thrill of making your mark on our world!

Thank you for being open to becoming a bigger game player. Please know that I'm an ally in all that you wish to create with your life. We're all connected.

As my Dad always said to me, and which remains my own compelling purpose, "When you look back in your final days, you don't want to say, 'I wish I had done more with my life.' Instead, you want to say, 'What a great ride that was!'"

Remember, bigger game players don't watch from the stands. We're on the field and in the game!

Have at it! Your bigger game has already begun! Fasten your seat belts; it's going to be a great ride. Life is all made up!

● ✖ ●

Play Your Bigger Game

Comfort *Zones*	Hunger	*Compelling* Purpose
ASSESS	**BOLD** Action	GULP
SUSTAIN ABILITY	Allies	Investment

At our first Bigger Game Expo, one of our attendees, who was new to The Bigger Game philosophy, became so inspired that she wrote the following poem that deeply captures the essence of what playing a bigger game is all about. Enjoy!

MY BIGGER GAME
A poem written by Niketa A. Coles
at The Bigger Game Expo, Silver Bay, NY
May 2013

WOW, Allies are truly here, there and everywhere.

The Investment is what we put into the game to show how much we care.

Comfort Zones are not always bad, and sometimes they should be embraced.

Bold Actions aren't that hard and can be done with grace.

A Compelling Purpose is when you know there is something you must do.

Now the GULP is scary, but take a deep breath and remember that I AM U!

And once you realize how much we are all the same,

Then Assessing yourself will never lead to shame or blame.

Hunger puts you in search of, and it's where the journey truly begins.

And Sustainability is when you know you're doing it for others . . .

each one, teach one, which never ends.

Now I wish I could tell you that I knew the name,

but I don't.

So for now I'll just call it My Bigger Game!

JOIN THE BIGGER GAME MOVEMENT

My Bigger Game is to activate millons of people around the world to play their own compelling Bigger Games.

Join The Bigger Game movement and become a Bigger Game player!

Visit www.RickTamlyn.com and www.BiggerGame.com to join our mailing list; share your own Bigger Game; and learn about future events, offers, and products.

EXPERIENCE THE BIGGER GAME

Are you interested in a deeper conversation about the concepts and material presented in this book? *Play Your Bigger Game* is available as an experiential keynote; a half-day introduction; a 2-day workshop; a 4-day retreat; and a customized experience to activate and inspire your employees, team, or organization.

Learn more at www.RickTamlyn.com and www.BiggerGame.com.

● ✖ ●

ACKNOWLEDGMENTS

I have always loved the phrase "It takes a village!" And this could not be more apropos in the creation of *Play Your Bigger Game*. I am so blessed to live and be loved in a very large global village. There are thousands of people from around the world who have touched my mind, my heart, and my soul. They are all part of the fabric of this book. I offer my deep gratitude to all of you.

In this village I am so blessed to have Shannon Marven, my literary agent at Dupree Miller & Associates, who saw the potential within me and then called it out and took it to a higher level than I could have imagined. I am forever grateful.

I have deep gratitude to my friend, Wes Smith, the writer who added zest and depth to my stories and made the game so accessible to so many. Thank you also for shepherding The Bigger Game to the perfect allies.

Adora English and Jess Ponce are two allies who get it. Thank you for guiding me and loving me through my neurotic, confusing moments and my sometimes-overwhelming expression of passionate ideas. Your coaching changes me!

To my Hay House family, particularly Reid Tracy and Patrick Gabrysiak, please know that it is an honor to be in a village with such brilliant thought leaders.

The Coaches Training Institute has been my home base for 20 years. I thank you all for waking me to my potential and guiding me to my leadership work in our world. You are my co-active "other" family—always have been, always will be.

To The Bigger Game trainers around the world, your dedication and love of this work matters so much. To know that at any given moment you are activating people in your world to play bigger games is an amazing feeling that I cherish. I appreciate you, admire you, and love you deeply. The movement is now real!

Looking at one's inner life is paramount to playing a Bigger Game out in the world. I thank Leza Danly, L.A. Reding, Dr. Don, and my first coach Cynthia Loy Darst, who help me unpack my humanity and my spiritual self and turn it into creativity to share with the world. Your deep love is a game changer.

To my dear personal family, thank you for letting me be me! More important, you love me as me. This unconditional love frees me to be open and accessible to the world, for I know there is always a place to go back to reground and recharge.

I thank my co-creator in this work and life partner, Chuck Lioi. You are the master of making dreams into reality, over and over, again and again. I continue to be in awe. I am blessed to have a magical career *and* to live in a magic house because of your magical skills. I love you!

Finally, to all of you who have allowed The Bigger Game to open up and expand your dreams, aspirations, and desires to new levels, I honor your courage, vulnerability, and commitment to impact your worlds in positive ways. *Thank you, thank you, thank you!* This is why I do this work—to activate the human potential, and express more of ourselves in service of a more engaged, alive, and connected world. May we see and support each other on The Bigger Game playing field somewhere in the world.

More to come!
Namaste,
Rick T.

● ✖ ●

ABOUT THE AUTHOR

Rick Tamlyn is a respected thought leader in the human-development field with a global audience from his work as a keynote speaker, workshop facilitator, and executive leadership coach. He teaches that our experiences, emotions, reactions, and relationships are made up—*life is all made up.*

Wielding his unique blend of wisdom, wit, and humor, Rick's keynotes and workshops are interactive, dynamic, and entertaining. He has presented his programs to individuals, teams, and Fortune 100 organizations in more than 17 countries.

In 2001, Rick co-created The Bigger Game: a tool that inspires people from all walks of life to get out of their comfort zones and invent the life they want. He has both inspired and challenged thousands of people and teams to achieve their personal and professional goals and up their game in service of a more fulfilled and sustainable world.

He is a Certified Professional Co-Active Coach (CPCC) and a Master Certified Coach (MCC) as designated by the International Coach Federation (ICF), and he also is a senior trainer for The Coaches Training Institute in San Francisco, a world-renowned coach-training and leadership-development organization.

Rick has a BA in communications from Hope College in Michigan and an MFA in acting from the University of Connecticut. He enjoys spending his free time boating and sailing on Lake George in upstate NY with his family and friends.

●　✖　●

We hope you enjoyed this Hay House book.
If you'd like to receive our online catalog featuring additional information on
Hay House books and products, or if you'd like to find out more about
the Hay Foundation, please contact:

Hay House, Inc., P.O. Box 5100, Carlsbad, CA 92018-5100
(760) 431-7695 or (800) 654-5126
(760) 431-6948 (fax) or (800) 650-5115 (fax)
www.hayhouse.com® • **www.hayfoundation.org**

✪ ✪ ✪

Published and distributed in Australia by:
Hay House Australia Pty. Ltd., 18/36 Ralph St., Alexandria NSW 2015 •
Phone: 612-9669-4299 • *Fax:* 612-9669-4144 • www.hayhouse.com.au

Published and distributed in the United Kingdom by:
Hay House UK, Ltd., Astley House, 33 Notting Hill Gate, London W11 3JQ •
Phone: 44-20-3675-2450 • *Fax:* 44-20-3675-2451 • www.hayhouse.co.uk

Published and distributed in the Republic of South Africa by:
Hay House SA (Pty), Ltd., P.O. Box 990, Witkoppen 2068 •
Phone/Fax: 27-11-467-8904 • www.hayhouse.co.za

Published in India by:
Hay House Publishers India, Muskaan Complex, Plot No. 3, B-2, Vasant Kunj,
New Delhi 110 070 • *Phone:* 91-11-4176-1620 •
Fax: 91-11-4176-1630 • www.hayhouse.co.in

Distributed in Canada by:
Raincoast, 9050 Shaughnessy St., Vancouver, B.C. V6P 6E5 •
Phone: (604) 323-7100 • *Fax:* (604) 323-2600 • www.raincoast.com

✪ ✪ ✪

Take Your Soul on a Vacation

Visit **www.HealYourLife.com®** to regroup, recharge,
and reconnect with your own magnificence.
Featuring blogs, mind-body-spirit news, and life-changing wisdom
from Louise Hay and friends.

Visit **www.HealYourLife.com** today!